# Finding Your Leadership Focus

# Finding Your Leadership Focus

## *What Matters Most for Student Results*

### Douglas B. Reeves

*Foreword by*
**Michael Fullan**

Teachers College
Columbia University
New York and London

The following materials are available for free download and printing
from the Teachers College Press website, www.tcpress.com:

- Figure 1.2, From Labels to Implementation, page 9
- Figure 6.1, Influence and Impact, page 53
- Figure 9.1, The Leadership Focus Assessment, pages 94–95
- Appendix B, PIM™ School Improvement Audit, pages 127–135
- Appendix E, Science Fair Reflections, pages 143–144

Published by Teachers College Press, 1234 Amsterdam Avenue, New York, NY 10027

Library of Congress Cataloging-in-Publication Data

Reeves, Douglas B., 1953–
    Finding your leadership focus : what matters most for student results /
Douglas B. Reeves ; foreword by Michael Fullan.
        p.   cm.
    Includes bibliographical references and index.
    ISBN 978-0-8077-5170-1 (pbk. : alk. paper)
    ISBN 978-0-8077-5171-8 (hardcover : alk. paper)
        1. Educational leadership.   2. Academic achievement.   I. Title.

    LB2806.R366 2011
    371.2—dc22                                                    2010031534

ISBN 978-0-8077-5170-1 (paper)
ISBN 978-0-8077-5171-8 (hardcover)

Printed on acid-free paper
Manufactured in the United States of America

18 17 16 15 14 13 12 11      8 7 6 5 4 3 2 1

# Contents

# Foreword

**D**OUG REEVES puts our feet to the fire when it comes to deep school improvement, and then he shows us how to handle it. *Finding Your Leadership Focus* takes all the excuses off the table and gives the reader clear and compelling ideas for action. Doug is a master of clarity, precision, and know-how in dealing with complex matters while rendering them manageable.

His Law of Initiative Fatigue is a painful but real wake-up call for us to stop trying to do everything. He shows how this law creeps into our everyday agenda and what to do about it. His chapter on "weeding the garden" is a gem of practical advice.

Reeves doesn't just tell us what not to do. His research is so carefully documented and so clearly argued that we see precisely what should be our focus. His three leadership essentials have such elegant precision: Effective leaders spend their time on focus and monitoring, and they have a strong sense of efficacy.

Reeves also clearly weaves back and forth from system level to classroom/school level. The cluster of three chapters on system focus, school focus, and how leaders can help teachers zero in on power standards is a complete guide to sustained action that has a proven track record for getting results.

All the way through this book are carefully documented findings, strategic action suggestions, insights, and instruments for improving leadership. His "leadership focus assessment" again is a simple but powerful aid to getting it right.

*Finding Your Leadership Focus* could not have arrived at a more timely moment in the history of reform. We have had punctuated decades of dramatic and urgent calls for system reform coupled with equally dramatic failures. *A Nation at Risk* (1983), Goals 2000 (1990), No Child Left Behind (2001), and now Race to the Top (2010) all paint a bleak picture, call for deep action, and sputter into the future. These national calls to action, including Race to the Top (so far), have not been able to achieve a core focus. They have not been able to focus on strategic actions that would mobilize scores of people at the school, district, state, and federal levels.

Doug Reeves's conclusions and agenda for action are exactly what is needed to change this sorry track record. My own recent experience in bringing about "whole system reform" has enabled me to understand what it takes to get success on a large scale (Fullan, 2010). Reeves takes us further and deeper into this critical territory. He does it with such elegance and relentless insistence that we are drawn—indeed, compelled— to want to take action. Read this book and "find *your* leadership focus." There is no time to waste, and there is plenty to gain.

—Michael Fullan

# Acknowledgments

I EXTEND MY DEEP APPRECIATION to Jean Ward of Teachers College Press for shepherding this project to its conclusion. The difference between this book as a concept and as a finished product is due to her belief in the project and her personal insight and perseverance. Cathy Shulkin edited the work and, as she has done with more than a dozen other books, brought order out of chaos. Brandon Doubek conducted the factor analysis upon which the research is based, and many of my colleagues at The Leadership and Learning Center contributed to the field observations and data gathering. Any merit in this book I happily share with them; responsibility for errors large and small remains my own.

## CHAPTER 1

# The Law of Initiative Fatigue

## Why Leadership Focus Matters

THERE WAS ONCE a splendid school leader who had many laudable intentions. The leader produced many outstanding initiatives, each of which was supported by solid research showing that the ideas had worked in other school systems. Each initiative was accompanied by thoughtful implementation plans requiring detailed documentation and by supporting professional development seminars and workshops. After each new workshop, the leader adopted appropriate supervision techniques, sometimes accompanied by technology that produced rich data, reports, charts, and graphs. As the year progressed, the leader noticed that the wonderful enthusiasm among teachers and administrators at the beginning of the year was being displaced by fatigue, resignation, anger, and despair. After all of the promising initiatives and hard work, the only thing this leader did not have was the desired results.

The bad news is that this story is hardly unique. The research on which this book is based includes an analysis of leadership initiatives in more than 2,000 schools in the United States and Canada. This research reveals that *initiative fatigue* is a serious and growing problem. By "initiative fatigue" I mean the tendency of educational leaders and policymakers to mandate policies, procedures, and practices that must be implemented by teachers and school administrators, often with insufficient consideration of the time, resources, and emotional energy required to begin and sustain the initiatives. Even the sturdiest bridges have load limits for a reason, as they can bear thousands of tons of weight up to a limit, with trucks, trains, and cars all crossing the bridges without incident. Once the load limit is exceeded, however, even a small additional weight can lead to catastrophic consequences.

Requirements for new initiatives almost always begin with a reasonable response to information that suggests that schools can improve their performance. Educational leaders develop programs—often in response to demands from policymakers—to improve literacy, citizenship, professional development, student health, data analysis, or instructional technology, or, without a hint of irony, they institute mandatory training to reduce faculty stress and burnout. When examined individually, each of these ideas might have merit. But when viewed as the final car on an overloaded bridge, even the most reasonable mandate can be the cause of initiative fatigue.

The point of this book is not to attack or defend any individual programs, but rather to equip leaders and policymakers with a method for establishing and maintaining leadership focus. Therefore, it is essential to note that initiative fatigue is not the result of malicious or feckless leadership. Indeed, it is the zeal of school leaders to serve the interest of students, as well as a host of governmental mandates that were equally well intentioned, that has led inexorably to the overwhelming number of initiatives that plague schools. The central thesis of this book is that leadership focus is a prerequisite for every other element of leadership. Specifically, leadership focus has the following characteristics: impact, leverage, and implementation. Let us briefly consider each of these criteria.

**IMPACT**   Leaders know that while perfection is elusive in educational research, we need not rely on guesswork or vendor claims. Hattie (2009) demonstrates convincingly in his examination of more than 800 meta-analyses including more than 83 million students that the claim that an initiative "works" is anemic and unpersuasive, because a comparison to "no impact" is a bar set so low that every initiative appears attractive. Impact worthy of leadership focus, he suggests, requires evidence that the benefit from a proposed initiative is significantly greater than the benefit that would arise from a continuation of present practice. Because 95% of interventions result in some gain in achievement, Hattie concludes, the criterion of "impact" must be more than "better than nothing." It must surpass a benchmark of real-world change.

**LEVERAGE**   Because there is invariably more demand than supply for the attention of leaders and teachers, leaders with focus choose those few initiatives that have leverage, that is, an impact on multiple variables.

For example, when schools increase their emphasis on nonfiction writing, the impact is visible not only in student literacy but also in student performance in math, science, and social studies (Reeves, 2002a). When teachers improve the accuracy, timeliness, and specificity of their feedback, it aids student learning in every endeavor (Hattie, 2009; Marzano, 2006). By contrast, leaders violate the principle of leverage when their response to lower science test scores is a flurry of science curriculum initiatives that divert time and attention from student literacy.

**IMPLEMENTATION**   Leaders who are serious about implementation create a continuum of performance, including introduction, initiation, application, and capacity building. This range of implementation is not overwhelming in its complexity, but it is far more meaningful than a binary approach that compares one program with another, or that compares the presence of a program with the absence of a program. Most program evaluations take this either/or approach because the evaluations assume that the most important impact on achievement is the presence of an instructional program rather than the degree to which that program is implemented. However, our research demonstrates that it is not the mere presence of a program that influences student achievement, but rather the ability of educational leaders to assess the degree of implementation of instructional initiatives and then use that information to improve implementation at every level.

## The Costs and Benefits of Focus

Without focus, even the best leadership ideas will fail, the most ideal research-based initiatives will fail, and the most self-sacrificing, earnest leaders will fail. Worst of all, without focus by educational leaders, students and teachers will fail.

Fortunately, there is good news as well. When school leaders find their focus, the rewards are rapid and significant. While focus alone is not a sufficient strategy for school improvement, focus is a prerequisite for improvement. Our multivariate analysis reveals that when focus is combined with other variables—such as effective monitoring, professional learning, assessment, and feedback—then student achievement gains are more than five times greater than when a failure of focus prevents successful teaching and leadership. This book will help leaders at every level—from teacher leaders to administrative leaders to board leaders and senior policymakers—find their focus. Readers will find not only a strong evidentiary basis to stop the madness of proliferating initiatives but also practical tools to evaluate alternatives, establish priorities, and "just say no" to the next recommended program idea that will, however well-intentioned, rob leaders, teachers, and students of the time and energy they require for effective learning.

## The Illogical Imperative: Do It All and Do It Now

"Don't just do something, stand there!" Although this counterintuitive advice is rare in the literature of leadership, it is far more sound than the litany of prescriptions that piles one idea on top of another, crushing school leaders, teachers, and ultimately students under the weight of too many seemingly attractive ideas. The impact of too many initiatives imposed on limited or declining reserves of time, resources, and emotional energy of staff members is shown in Figure 1.1, which illustrates the Law of Initiative Fatigue. The horizontal axis represents the number of new and continuing initiatives; the vertical axis represents the impact of those initiatives on student achievement. The line on the graph is seductive, as it begins by showing, however briefly, a rise in impact as the initial initiatives are implemented. Schools without writing programs, for example, show striking benefits from an increase in writing, particularly when the programs focus on nonfiction writing skills, such as description, analysis, and persuasion (Reeves, 2002a). Schools with incoherent or nonexistent reading, math, or discipline programs similarly benefit when there is some order imposed on the chaos. However, it does not follow that if implementing the first program is good, then adding seventh, eighth, and ninth programs is better. In fact, after the initial brief positive impact, the effectiveness of adding programs declines precipitously.

Inevitably, this graph elicits a skeptical response: "It's not the quantity of the initiatives that matters, but the quality," the critics claim. That would seem logical, at least in theory. But in practice, the quantity of initiatives creates a "crowding out" effect that inhibits the effectiveness of even the best programs. The instigators of initiative fatigue defend the quality of each individual initiative without recognizing the consequences

**FIGURE 1.1**   The Law of Initiative Fatigue

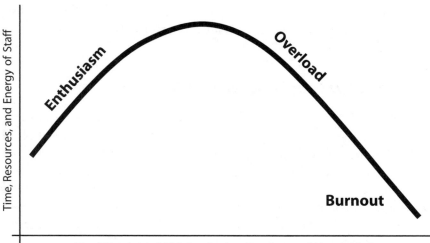

Total Number of Old, Continuing, Pending, and New Initiatives

of the cumulative burdens they place on teachers and administrators. In our review of school improvement plans for this book, we found that sometimes initiative fatigue was a response to a mandate at the state or system level. Schools were required to show evidence that staff members were trained in legally mandated topics, typically involving safety, labor practices, and professional conduct. Deficiencies in previous accreditation visits led to the expectation of a one-to-one correspondence between each deficiency and a bullet point in the plan to address it. Community expectations in strategic planning meetings yielded dozens of expectations for schools to respond to stakeholder needs. Such conditions are why leadership focus is rare. Political and regulatory realities militate against focus and in favor of fragmentation.

While the forces driving initiative fatigue may be politically popular—encouraging school leaders to resign themselves to the notion that they are responsive to a variety of external demands—the fragmentation comes at a high cost, and it is worth applying the necessary will and political dexterity to resist. In the schools studied for the research described in this book, only 0.57%—one half of one percent—of schools achieved the highest scores on the "focus" variable, meaning that they had six or fewer claimed priorities. The other 99.5% of schools far exceeded this manageable number. How significant is this challenge? In our research, we found a single school with 77 separate initiatives and a district with 246 distinct initiatives. With eerie similarity, both the school and the district leaders with these dubious records described their laundry lists as "strategic priorities," casting doubt on both the terms "strategy" and "priority."

## Does Initiative Fatigue Affect Your Schools?

If you believe that I am overstating the case, take this simple test. Divide a piece of paper into two columns. In the left-hand column, list all of the new initiatives your school, district, or system has begun in the past 24 months. In the right-hand column, list the programs that have been examined carefully and terminated. If the right-hand column exceeds the left-hand column, then you have just won dinner, on me, at the best Indian restaurant in Salem, Massachusetts. The odds, however, are against you, as this challenge has already been presented to 160 groups with a collective participation of more than 8,000 educators and school leaders. Never—not once—has the right-hand column exceeded the left-hand column.

Let us assume that every single initiative in the left-hand column stemmed from the best of motives. Who could possibly be opposed to better reading, writing, math, character development, social action, economic literacy, time management, personal responsibility, personal fitness, diet and exercise, consumer awareness, programs on date rape or alcohol and drug addiction, or community service? This list is at only 14 common initiatives, and it is not difficult to see how the first one, "reading," could be long forgotten. The advocates of all of these initiatives never intended that their proposals would diminish any other initiative of equal or greater value, and they certainly never intended to harm the entire system. But as the Law of Initiative Fatigue suggests, no deliberate hierarchy of quality or impact governs the way most schools juggle initiatives. The latest priority diminishes the time, resources, and emotional energy that are devoted to the previous priorities. The causes of this dilemma are not malice, but institutional fragmentation.

## Causes of Initiative Fatigue

The "Do It All and Do It Now" imperative stems from both institutional and individual sources. Institutional sources include both planning and financial policies. Planning policies arise from national, state, provincial, and local policies that have unquestionably meritorious intent. "Every school will have a plan for student safety" seems benign. But whatever schools eventually develop is never enough, and soon each school must have a plan for everything from crosswalk safety to inhalants in the workplace to blood-borne pathogens.

The implementation regulations associated with these requirements, none of which are apocryphal, lead to the absurd spectacle of teachers and administrators sitting in dark auditoriums listening to a lecture about blood-borne pathogens for 20 minutes—not 19 or 21, but the mandated 20—while they could be in their classrooms getting ready for students who need their care and attention the next day. I have asked policymakers responsible for these sorts of regulations if they would consider testing the hypothesis that their regulations actually led to the results they sought. In brief, the answer was "No—and you cannot possibly be suggesting that we have requirements that are not in the best interests of students, can you?"

In fact, this challenge is precisely the focus of this book. The institutional imperative to mandate the publication of plans and goals stems from good motives but poor research. It substitutes documents for decisions; it values paper over progress; it values responsiveness to bureaucratic authority over results. The conclusion of the research I will describe is not that leadership and authority are inherently bad. The response to this challenge requires not anarchy, but analysis.

## Forces Against Focus:
## Politics, Bureaucracy, and Culture

Schmoker (2004) makes a compelling argument that school systems are political entities that are conditioned to place plans ahead of action. He asks the "Dr. Phil" question that every teacher, school leader, and policymaker must ask: Is it working? If more of X—a particular practice or policy—yields more of Y—a definable positive impact on students—then we can answer that question in the affirmative. For example, if both the scientific literature and personal experience suggest that more diet and exercise yield more weight loss and physical fitness, then we might conclude accurately that the former leads to the latter. It is therefore not unreasonable to ask whether every mandate from a federal, state, or local school system is related to the goals of the system. The presumption of strategic planning, for example, is that the structure imposed by a plan yields definable actions by teachers and administrators which, in turn, result in actions by students which, in turn, result in improved academic performance. These are entirely reasonable assumptions—at least as reasonable as the assumptions that heavy objects fall to earth more rapidly than light objects, that the seasons are caused by the distance of the orbit of earth from the sun, or that the sun is the center of the universe. But all of these very reasonable assumptions have been tested and found inaccurate based on the observations of those researchers willing to challenge prevailing wisdom.

Nameless bureaucracy is not the only force working against leadership focus. There are also strong political and cultural predispositions that favor diffusion over focus. The best illustration of this is the preponderance of initiative fatigue in high-poverty schools which, in the United States, are defined as Title I schools, based on the high percentage of their student population eligible for free or reduced-priced lunch.

While Title I funds are allocated from the federal government based upon student poverty levels, changes in school needs and student population characteristics mean that the amount of available Title I funds is inconsistent from one year to the next. This is particularly true of the $100 billion in federal "stimulus funds" allocated to school systems in the summer of 2009. The funds available then may never be available again. The result of this funding inconsistency is an institutional incentive to use these federal funds not for enduring long-term practices, but rather for short-term programs. But if we have learned anything in our research, it is that practices endure while programs fade. One way to test whether your school is focused on definable practices or merely the label of a program is to complete the exercise shown in Figure 1.2.

In a meeting, start by identifying some initiative that you have reason to believe is widely and consistently used in your system. Then ask people in the meeting to work entirely alone, without any conversation or collaboration, to complete the document. No one need put their name on the paper, as the purpose is not to make an example of any individual in the group, but rather to recognize that there is a difference between the *label* of an initiative and the *practices* that are actually applied in the classroom. Program labels are particularly unhelpful. Terms such as "differentiated instruction," "balanced literacy," and "professional learning communities" are used profligately to describe a wide range of professional

**FIGURE 1.2**   From Labels to Implementation

**STEP 1:** Working as a group, identify some of the most important initiatives in your school or system. Agree upon one initiative that the group believes is widely and consistently used in your system.

Write the name of that instructional initiative here:

*For the rest of this exercise, please work entirely alone, without collaboration with any colleagues. Please do not put your name on the paper or otherwise identify yourself, your grade level, or your school.*

**STEP 2:** Answer the following questions about the initiative identified in Step 1.

• How much instructional time do you spend on this initiative every day?

• If students are not mastering the concept you are teaching in this initiative, how much extra time do you devote to those students every day?

• If you were observing a classroom teacher to assess the degree to which this initiative is being effectively implemented, what would you look for if you made a brief (4–5 minute) visit to the classroom and focused exclusively on looking for the *three most important things* that would show evidence of effective implementation:

(1)

(2)

(3)

Make a prediction about the consistency of your implementation compared with that of your colleagues, with a score of "10" representing very consistent implementation and a score of "1" representing very inconsistent implementation.

For this particular instructional initiative, I predict that the consistency of implementation among **classroom teachers** is:

1   2   3   4   5   6   7   8   9   10

For this particular instructional initiative, I predict that the consistency of implementation among **building administrators** is:

1   2   3   4   5   6   7   8   9   10

For this particular instructional initiative, I predict that the consistency of implementation among **central office administrators** is:

1   2   3   4   5   6   7   8   9   10

**STEP 3:** Post your anonymous responses to these questions and discuss with your colleagues the similarities and differences you observe in defining implementation.

This figure is available for free download and printing from www.tcpress.com.

practices. In the pages that follow, you will learn the value of moving from the use of generic labels to describe professional practices to the application of explicit descriptions of professional behaviors.

The distinction between labels and practices can be stark. Consider the example of a popular literacy initiative. In three school systems with more than 130 schools, I explored the degree of consistency in the application of their reading initiative. Principals and faculty members knew the name of the literacy initiative and they all asserted confidently that it was "universally applied and non-negotiable." But when I asked about the details of implementation, a different picture emerged. The time allocated for the "universally applied" program ranged from 45 minutes to 3 hours. The "top five strategies" represented by the "non-negotiable" program varied widely. Even when the strategies were similar, the definition of basic terms, such as "guided reading" and "independent reading," varied widely from classroom to classroom and school to school. If you want to begin to challenge initiative fatigue in your school, you must start with a widespread recognition that we must focus on practices, not programs, to gain deep implementation.

## The Good News: Change Is Possible

If any silver lining has been revealed in the research thus far, it is that change is possible. With a population that included largely the same students, same parents, and same teachers, over the 3-year course of the study we observed schools increase by dramatic proportions their scores on the "focus" variable, and as they did so, their student results improved. While in the first year of the study only one half of one percent of schools achieved the highest scores on focus, by the third year more than 10% had achieved that score—a 20-fold increase in an objective evaluation of focus. Best of all, the schools that showed dramatic improvements in focus also showed the best gains in achievement in reading, math, science, and social studies.

This school-level improvement is particularly encouraging, because political support for initiative proliferation is strong. It would be tempting to claim that in order to defeat initiative fatigue, national, state, and provincial leaders and policymakers must first get focused themselves.

After all, such reasoning goes, it is the politicians who have fueled the unending stream of programs and requirements, and we cannot expect that any school or classroom will be more focused than the leaders and policymakers. But the evidence tells a different story. Schools in the same district—and with the same state legislature and the same school board and the same list of requirements—can make dramatic improvements in their own level of focus and, as a result, can have a positive impact on student achievement. Of course it would be better if state and national policymakers would also take this advice to heart. In the meantime, however, every educator and school leader reading this book can take immediate action to improve focus and defeat initiative fatigue. We need not wait for perfect alignment of national policies and systems to make significant improvements. We can do it now.

When time, resources, and leadership energy are constant or declining, each new initiative receives fewer minutes, fewer dollars, and less leadership attention. The rest of this book explains how schools can defy the Law of Initiative Fatigue and the consequences that result when leaders fail to focus.

## CHAPTER 2

# The Research

WHEN CONFRONTED with research claims in education, teachers and school leaders have learned to be skeptical consumers. Published claims can be wildly inconsistent, with different authors presenting credible cases for significantly different conclusions. Recent examples include debates about the value of homework, the relative impact of school and demographic factors on student performance, and the effects of alternative grading systems on student achievement. At other times, research claims are exaggerated, asserting that the impact of an instructional program is significant when, in fact, it is simply a little better than if a student had stayed away from school. And in many cases, claims about the impact of teaching and leadership are based upon anecdotal experience and do not reflect a systematic measurement of student achievement. Therefore, in presenting the research for this book, I wish first to acknowledge the reasonability of a skeptical perspective and address some of the most common challenges directly. Most importantly, as the references at the end of the book make clear, the research presented in this volume should be viewed in the context of the work of other researchers and, in the end, readers should consider not a single study but the preponderance of the evidence as they make decisions about their own teaching and leadership practices.

For the purposes of this chapter, let us consider the questions that practitioners raise: Is the research consistent? Are the claims reasonable? Is the research relevant to student achievement?

First, consider the issue of consistency of the research on leadership focus. While it is not difficult to find authors who find merit in leadership focus (Fullan, 2009, 2010; Kotter, 2008; Schmoker, 2006), it is equally easy to find exhaustive prescriptions for multiple simultaneous instructional and leadership initiatives. Hattie (2009) suggests that there is evidence for effectiveness of the following—and this is only a partial list:

| | |
|---|---|
| Self-questioning | Second/third chance |
| Meta-cognitive strategies | Phonics instruction |
| Peer tutoring | Vocabulary instruction |
| Formative evaluation | Microteaching |
| Mastery learning | Small group learning |
| Concept mapping | Reciprocal teaching |
| Advance organizers | Direct instruction |
| Writing programs | Interactive video |

Although this book provides new and previously unpublished findings about the power of leadership focus, the research is consistent with three recent surveys of leadership impact on student achievement. Hattie (2009) found that specific decisions of leaders with regard to assessment, curriculum, and feedback had disproportionate impacts on student results. His examination of more than 800 meta-analyses provides the largest extant collection of research on student achievement. Marzano and Waters (2009) found that district-level leadership had measurable impacts on student achievement, and discovered that the greatest impact was associated with simultaneous "loose–tight" leadership strategies, in which leaders allowed schools and teachers discretion in some areas, provided that there were diligent controls on the classroom and administrative matters that had the greatest impact on student learning. Marzano, Waters, and McNulty (2005) concurred that building-level leadership could be directly linked to effective teaching and, in turn, student results.

Second, teachers and educational leaders who consider research claims want to know if those claims are reasonable or exaggerated. The search for the elusive "silver bullet" remains unburdened by the evidence that the object of the search does not exist. Consider the cringe-inducing claim of advertisements that "students who used our program gained 20% in test scores in 3 months!" The implication is that there is a single cause or a single effect and that the mere presence of a program was the only cause for the gain in test scores. By the same logic, the trees that grew, the flowers that bloomed, and the babies that were born in proximity to the school also were the result of the same program that caused the 20% gain in test scores. This book focuses on more reasonable claims, because at the heart of the research is a multivariate analysis. In other words, there is hardly ever a single cause for a single effect, particularly in education. Rather, educational effects stem from the confluence of different variables—teaching, leadership, curriculum, and feedback—that occur simultaneously. It is not reasonable to claim that "our curriculum caused a 20% gain in achievement!" It *is* potentially reasonable to claim that "the application of this curriculum, along with effective feedback, skillful teaching, and focused leadership, was consistently associated with a 20% gain in student achievement." Even such a comparatively reasonable claim does not guarantee future results or establish a scientific link between cause and effect. But it certainly is more credible than the claims of many advertisements.

Third, readers reasonably wish to know if the research is relevant to student achievement. Do the claims represent merely the personal experiences of the author, or do they reveal a systematic relationship between teaching and leadership actions and student achievement? The research design employed in this study meets the standard that Marzano et al. (2005) established in that the variables under consideration represent 3 years of student achievement data in a variety of different subjects at the elementary, middle school, and high school levels.

This book is addressed to an audience of practitioners and policymakers, and therefore I have attempted to present the data in an accessible manner in the main text. Appendix A contains more of the technical details of the study. For researchers and academics who may wish to have access to even more detailed information, the complete data set and all of the graphs used in the analysis are available for free download from The Leadership and Learning Center (www.LeadandLearn.com), an organization devoted to the sharing of educational research. The questions that all readers have, of course, focus on the validity, reliability, and limitations of the research, and this chapter will briefly address those matters.

## How the Research Was Conducted

The PIM™ (Planning, Implementation, and Monitoring) studies were based on double-blind reviews of more than 2,000 schools in the United States and Canada. By "double-blind" I mean that two separate researchers evaluate the school plans and practices based on a rubric created by

The Leadership and Learning Center (see Appendix B) and come to the same conclusion at least 80% of the time. After the initial scoring, the assessors engage in a collaborative process, often referred to as "moderation," that is commonly used in assessing student performance in writing, demonstration, or other performances that are not amenable to numerical description. In order to have greater consistency and reliability in scoring, it is essential for the evaluators to address their disagreements openly. In some cases, the disagreement is due to a differing interpretation of the scoring rubric. In those cases, the evaluators must stop, confer, and improve the clarity of the rubric.

The participants in this sample were voluntary, not random. Therefore, we cannot claim that they represent all schools, any more than the polls that predicted the victories of presidential candidates Al Gore or Thomas Dewey were able to predict accurate results for those elections. Any sample, random or nonrandom, must contain errors, and this one is no exception. But the sample is large, including more than 2,000 schools with more than 1.5 million students, and diverse. It includes high- and low-poverty schools, high- and low-second-language schools, and schools from urban, suburban, and rural environments.

## Experimental Versus Quasi-Experimental Research

Research on human subjects, including psychological, educational, and medical research, suffers from many limitations, some of which are careless but at least a few of which are deliberate. The primary limitation of most research is the failure to have double-blind random assignment of subjects to experimental and control groups (Campbell & Stanley, 1963). The gold standard in medical research, for example, is that neither cancer patients nor the people who evaluate the efficacy of their treatments know whether they received the real drug or surgical procedure (the experimental group) or received a placebo (the control group). This sort of rigorous investigation can reveal some strikingly counterintuitive findings, such as the results of recent studies that revealed that many heart and knee surgeries that consumed billions of dollars of expense and caused a great deal of pain and suffering in patients yielded results that were indistinguishable from "procedures" that appeared to be surgeries but were illusory (Patterson, Grenny, Maxfield, McMillan, & Switzler, 2008).

As someone who has undergone painful and recurring knee surgery, these results are fascinating to me. Nevertheless, I cannot help but be thankful that I was not one of the subjects in these particular experiments. Certainly I would not want to be the patient with terminal cancer who was receiving the placebo in order to prove that the treatment provided to another randomly chosen patient who received the real drug was effective. Similarly, I would not want my child to be randomly assigned to a classroom without any reading program or with an ineffective reading program, simply to enable the children of other parents to benefit, by the luck of the draw, from an effective reading program. The technical research term that describes parents and patients like me is "selfish," and I plead guilty as charged.

As a researcher, I am unwilling to impose on the children of other parents that which I am unwilling to accept for my own children. Researchers have not always demonstrated this kind of concern for human subjects. In the past, distinguished scientists in the infamous Tuskegee studies deliberately denied treatment to African American men who had syphilis. Medical science advanced, to our shame, based on what we learned from that research. Psychologists and sociologists learned a great deal from Stanley Milgram's seminal *Obedience to Authority* (1974) studies, but we should also be grateful that universities now have Human Subjects Review Boards that balance the intent of the researcher with the very real impact on the people who are the subjects of investigation. In one of Milgram's studies, research subjects were instructed to administer doses of electricity to other subjects (who were, in fact, confederates of the researchers) when the other subjects responded incorrectly to questions. Even as the respondents writhed in pain in response to the fake jolt of electricity, the research subjects continued to comply with the instructions of the researchers. The grim conclusion was that normal, law-abiding, nice people were capable of inflicting great pain on others, provided that they were responding to an authority figure. I described these ethical dilemmas in the article "Galileo's Dilemma" (Reeves, 2002b), in which I attempted to explain why ethical obligations to children trump our pursuit of experimental rigor. The text of that commentary is presented in Appendix C.

Fortunately, there is an alternative to double-blind random assignment as a research technique, and that is the examination of data retrospectively in "quasi-experimental" groups. Because we are evaluating groups that were not randomly assigned and were established before our inquiry began, our research lacks the rigor of a true experimental design. But that does not render it valueless. Some of the most important research of the past century is the result of a backward look at the data. For example, the essential research on the link between cigarette smoking and lung cancer was the result of quasi-experimental designs. People were not randomly assigned to the "Marlboro Man" group or the "Clean Living Smoke-Free" group. Rather, researchers noted a correlation between people who died of lung cancer and those who smoked. The next time you hear research dismissed as "only correlation, not causation," remember that this was precisely the argument advanced by the American Tobacco Institute in support of the proposition that cigarette smoking was actually healthy. This absurd reasoning had a number of prominent advocates, including such movie stars as Ronald Reagan, John Wayne, and Al Jolson.

In the present study, we did not randomly assign students to schools with good leadership focus and bad leadership focus. We simply evaluated a large number of schools with different characteristics and different student results, and sought to consider the puzzle of which causes were related to which effects. Certainly, there are exceptions that test the rule. My paternal grandmother and maternal grandfather smoked like chimneys and lived into their nineties. That is not necessarily an advertisement for tobacco consumption, but rather the essential research point that the standard for research is not perfection, but the preponderance of the evidence. For the matter at hand, there are certainly schools with many initiatives that succeed despite their schizophrenic leadership, and there are highly focused schools that fail. However, on the whole, the bulk of the evidence supports leadership focus. If the only two lessons you take from this chapter are "don't smoke, and focus your school leadership," then your conclusions result from research that is adequate, but not perfect.

## Multivariate Versus Two-Variable Analysis

When I taught graduate statistics and research classes many years ago, I used to ask my students to master at least two concepts. The first is that not everything that matters can be measured numerically. While musicologists have often tried to infer mathematical order from the music of Johann Sebastian Bach, a focus on measurement rather than majesty, wonder, and brilliance risks dilution of the pure enjoyment of his music.

The second lesson is that life is multivariate; there is hardly ever one cause for one effect. Continuing the previous examples, it is true that diet and exercise lead to better cardiac health and smoking leads to cancer. But many other factors, including genetic predispositions, work and home environments, maternal health during pregnancy, stress, and a host of other variables also influence heart disease and cancer. In considering educational strategies, we know that leadership decision-making is profoundly influential (Goodlad, 1984) and teacher quality is an essential variable (Darling-Hammond, 2000). But it would be foolish to ignore the impact of home language, poverty, medical care, housing, and other influences on achievement (Rothstein, 2004a, 2004b).

Because so many different factors are at work in influencing student achievement, how is it possible to identify the relative impact of a single variable? The most direct method of making such an assessment is to change just one variable at a time. Ideally, a researcher could compare two groups of schools that are identical in every respect—same teacher quality, same leadership quality, same budgets, same student demographic characteristics, and so forth—with only *one* important variable that is different—such as a different schoolwide reading program. Then, in theory, we could draw the inference that differences in student achievement between the two groups were not the result of teaching, leadership, or student demographics, but solely the result of the different reading program.

In the real world, however, it is difficult to hold variables constant in parallel samples in order to study the impact of a single variable. Multivariate analysis is a tool that helps us do that, but it is essentially no more than a way of studying a hierarchy of relationships between variables. For example, a multivariate analysis of causes of student achievement might consider a combination of variables, including attendance, curriculum, and assessment. While all of these independent variables are important, attendance is more important than others, because when students fail to attend school, they are not able to benefit from the other teaching variables under consideration. It does not reveal causes, even though researchers use terms like "independent variable" that are associated with causes and "dependent variable" that are associated with effects. The truth is that we are hypothesizing which is the chicken and which is the egg. The multivariate analysis only reveals relationships, not causality.

Although I am acknowledging the limitations of multivariate techniques or, for that matter, any analytical technique that depends upon statistical correlation, I am not concluding that these techniques are valueless. Indeed, the great advantage of multivariate analysis is that it allows us to identify things that are related to different degrees. Linda Darling-Hammond's critically important multivariate analysis of student demographics and teaching quality revealed that all of the variables were related, but that teaching quality had a significantly greater impact on student achievement than did the other variables (Haycock, 1998). Multivariate analysis also forces us to acknowledge that there is variation that is simply not explained and thus liberates us from the facile "one cause for one effect" implication of two-variable analysis. For example, Darling-Hammond's (2000) analysis suggested that 49% of variation in student achievement was explained by teacher quality factors and 24% was explained by student demographic characteristics. That leaves 27% of variation unexplained. The model is not perfect—it is rare that causes under study explain 100% of the variation in effects—but this analysis nevertheless provides important insights for researchers and policymakers. Moreover, multivariate techniques are vastly superior to the assumptions of two-variable correlation analysis, which too often are presented as cause and effect and which fail to recognize the important impacts of many other variables in the equation of life.

## The Standard of Evidence in Educational Research

Because children's future learning opportunities are influenced by the decisions they make, educational leaders and practitioners should have a high standard for the research they consider. However, this is far different from a standard of perfection, which is both impossible and has adverse policy consequences. When we consider recommendations for leadership focus in this book, for example, the question to be considered is not, "Can you prove to me that it will work every time?" I certainly cannot. Even the most sound educational and leadership practices are not effective with every student, but we use them anyway because the preponderance of the evidence suggests that they are effective. Consider the data displayed in Figure 2.1. This is a scatter plot representing student achievement in mathematics on the vertical axis and student

**FIGURE 2.1**    Writing Is Related to Higher Math Achievement

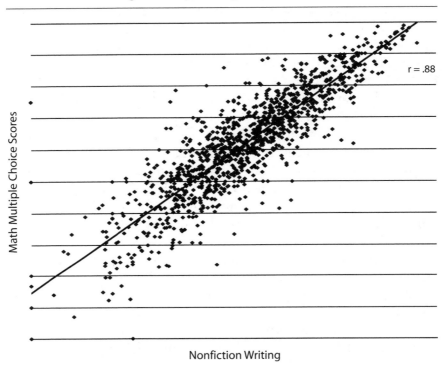

Nonfiction Writing

proficiency in nonfiction writing on the horizontal axis. It demonstrates that there is a very strong relationship between student performance in these two areas.

Since the data shown in Figure 2.1 were gathered, I have collected similar data for which the vertical axis represents student achievement in science, social studies, and other disciplines, and the link to writing remains very strong. I have changed the measurement on the horizontal axis from student proficiency in writing to student frequency of writing, and again the relationship remains almost identical—a Pearson correlation coefficient quite close to +0.8.

Look carefully at the graph. You will see that most of the points, representing the performance of individual students, are close to the line and conform to the general relationship between math and writing. Note, however, the points in the upper left-hand quadrant, which represent students who are doing well in math but not well in writing. And in the lower right-hand quadrant, we see points representing some students who clearly devoted a great deal of time and energy to writing, but whose efforts did not pay off in better math scores. These students represent outliers: that is, they do not conform to the general relationship between two variables observed in the population as a whole. There is nothing wrong with that. Perhaps you are an outlier, or, if not, then chances are you are or have been married to one. Outliers are neither good nor bad, but they are important in how they make us consider evidence from research.

Let us assume that you are faced with a decision. Students in your school are not performing well in math and you have concluded that you must increase the amount of instructional time they receive in this subject. When you look at all of the evidence in Figure 2.1, which cases will you find most persuasive when you have to make a practical decision about how to allocate time? Should you cut back on time allocated for writing in order to improve student achievement in math? If you focus on the vast majority of students, you might conclude that achievement in nonfiction writing and math, both of which require critical thinking and analysis, are so strongly related that taking away from one to "help" the other is not a wise strategy. If you focus on the outliers, you will come to a different conclusion.

Consider a somewhat more emotional topic, such as grading policy. The evidence strongly suggests that when the consequence for a student missing work is changed from receiving a zero to being required to complete the work, student achievement soars, failures decline, and student discipline improves dramatically (Guskey & Bailey, 2001; Marzano, 2006; Reeves, 2006a). Yet the most benign suggestions for improving grading policies are met with angry opposition from teachers, parents, and professors. The opposition to changes in grading policies is invariably focused on outliers—"I've tried that idea, and it didn't work for *that* kid." This argument may be right on the facts—perhaps the policy did not work for that student—but it is wrong on the logic and conclusion.

Being right on the facts but wrong on the logic can have tragic consequences. Some readers will recall the 1950s, when they knew of students or neighbors afflicted by polio. Some wore braces while others lived with the assistance of an iron lung. The nation engaged in a massive effort to vaccinate every citizen against polio and today, at least in North

America, the disease has been largely eliminated. Approximately 1 in every 25,000 children who receives the polio vaccine will get the disease, causing unbelievable heartache for the child and family. Some other vaccines carry similar, very small but very real, risks. As a result of a typhus vaccination, I was hospitalized for 3 days with symptoms related to the typhoid fever I was seeking to avoid. Based on the data, what decision will you make? What decision do you want other parents to make? Whatever you decide for yourself and your children, chances are that you certainly will want me and my children to get vaccinations, because that will reduce the risk of disease for the entire community, including you and your children. In other words, however compelling the outliers may be, we must make our policy decisions based on the weight of the evidence. It is tragic when a child has polio, and the hallucinations, fever, and other unpleasant symptoms of typhoid fever are no picnic either. But both are better alternatives to a society in which preventable disease becomes pervasive.

The standard of evidence, therefore, is not perfection. The standard is the weight of the available evidence. In the context of education, we should ask questions such as:

- Is the sample diverse, including schools that have both high and low populations of poor, minority, second language, and special education students?
- Is there a mix of research methods, including quantitative and qualitative studies?
- Are the findings consistent with those of other researchers? If there are inconsistencies, what makes this research more persuasive?

The answers to these questions do not yield perfection, but rather a more subtle understanding of how practitioners and policymakers choose among competing recommendations.

## Weighing Risks

Goldilocks does not inhabit the world of education. There is no "just right" in educational research, but rather the choice between two types of errors. Researchers typically have referred to these errors as Type I and Type II errors, referring, respectively, to the error in which we confirm a hypothesis that is untrue, and the error in which we fail to confirm a hypothesis that is true. While we can reduce these errors by equipping ourselves with larger sample sizes and conveniently consistent data sets, we can never eliminate them.

From a practical perspective, educational leaders make decisions about Type I and Type II errors every day, even if they do not use that terminology. If, for example, we are considering a shift of resources to improve literacy for eighth-grade students, we face two possible risks. The first is the risk that the literacy intervention is not effective or necessary for some students, and thus the time, money, and teaching talent invested in the literacy program will be wasted, and other programs from which those resources are diverted will be unnecessarily impaired. The second risk is that, as we wait for more perfect research findings, we fail to provide the intervention that eighth-grade students desperately need and send them to high school doomed to failure and on a path toward becoming dropouts, accompanied by a lifetime of adverse consequences for themselves, their families, and society.

Every resource allocation decision confronts these trade-offs—the costs of action compared with the costs of inaction. The conclusion should not be that we let the fear of adverse consequences lead us into pursuing every appealing initiative. Rather, we must consider the preponderance of the evidence, acknowledge that every decision contains error and risk, and then choose wisely. For the practicing school leader, this means making difficult choices from among competing alternatives. Five different choices in reading programs or technology vendors may all appear to have value, but an attempt to implement all of them simultaneously will rob the leader of the time to focus on one alternative that is essential to sustain it successfully. Rejection of the other four alternatives carries the risk that the leader will miss out on a good strategy. Failure to reject the other four alternatives will, by contrast, guarantee that an optimal strategy will not be given the time, professional energy, and leadership focus essential for success.

## CHAPTER 3

# The Essential Cluster of Leadership Practices

L EADERS ARE FACED with an avalanche of legitimate competing priorities that make it difficult to focus in a disciplined way. With this in mind, in our study we sought to understand where leaders placed their priorities and how persistent and pervasive was the loss of focus experienced by overloaded leaders, and the implications for student achievement. The evidence discussed in this chapter demonstrates that the cost of leadership diffusion is high and the rewards of leadership focus are great.

## Competing Demands on Leadership Attention

Leaders face three distinct types of demands for their attention: programs, processes, and practices. We have already explored the damage inflicted as a result of the Law of Initiative Fatigue, in which programs proliferate and ultimately overwhelm the available time, resources, and emotional energy of the leaders and teachers. In one elementary school, for example, we observed seven separate literacy programs, all competing for teacher attention within the same 90-minute literacy block.

Processes—such as teacher evaluation, data analysis, and the completion of required reports—also compete for leadership time and attention. Unfortunately, some of these processes elevate compliance over substantive leadership. For example, one district distributed a model building plan that was dutifully copied by some principals, who simply cut and pasted sections of the model plan, including descriptions of processes for grade levels that were not represented in their particular schools.

Many processes are driven by policy, law, or labor agreements. Legislation and administrative regulations in some states require leaders to create written plans, establish goals, and monitor performance on a dizzying array of topics, from student achievement and safety to worker safety and blood-borne pathogens. Each requirement, when considered individually, made sense at the time it was established. But, collectively, the weight of the process requirements placed on school leaders is counterproductive. The mandatory 20-minute "training" on blood-borne pathogens alluded to earlier is interspersed among a dozen other announcements to a preoccupied group of teachers and administrators, very few of whom find the instruction illuminating. While it is easy to blame legislators and school boards for burdensome processes, educators and their professional associations sometimes bear equal responsibility for the consequent failure in leadership focus. Collective bargaining agreements may restrict how leaders make use of time in faculty meetings and how administrators provide feedback to teachers. Research on the value of leaders providing effective monitoring and feedback for teachers is irrelevant if leaders are distracted by other policy priorities or subject to grievances when they pursue effective practices. Some restrictions on leadership are the result of inappropriate generalizations. In some jurisdictions, only the principal is permitted to conduct teacher observations and evaluations, whether the staff includes 20 teachers or 200. Such a requirement undermines effective replication of the best professional practices and limits the frequency and impact of observations of teaching practice.

One of the most pervasive results of leadership diffusion is the increasing reliance of educational administrators on prescribed programs that claim to be "teacher-proof." The leader need not engage in thoughtful interaction with professional educators if the only question is whether the teacher "delivered" the program, an observation that could be applied with equal rigor to the person who delivers textbooks, computer programs, or furniture. Leaders who assess delivery of programs have a relatively easy chore, evaluating by a brief observation and checklist. Leaders who assess the implementation of practices, by contrast, face a more complex challenge, one that requires more than a cursory visit but instead entails multiple observations. If there is a theme to the research on leadership impact, it is that "practices, not programs" are the key to developing and sustaining a high level of impact.

## Clusters of Effective Leadership Practices

We have found three essential clusters of leadership practices that positively impact student achievement: focus, monitoring, and efficacy (Figure 3.1). By "focus" we mean that leaders identify and monitor no more than six priority instructional initiatives that are linked clearly to specific student needs. By "monitoring" we mean the regular (typically at least once per quarter) systematic observation of adult actions—what teachers and leaders do in order to improve student learning. By "efficacy" we mean the personal conviction of teachers and administrators that their actions are the primary influences on the academic success of students.

   While "focus" sounds appealing to the overwhelmed leader, the inevitable question is, "focus on *what*?" Our research suggests that the "what" question must be preceded by the far more important issue of how leaders focus. Once a cluster of effective practices is identified, then the "what" question will be resolved based upon the needs of a particular school in a particular year. Sometimes the target for focus may be safety and discipline, other times reading comprehension, other times student engagement, and other times parent involvement.

**FIGURE 3.1**   Clusters of Effective Leadership Practices

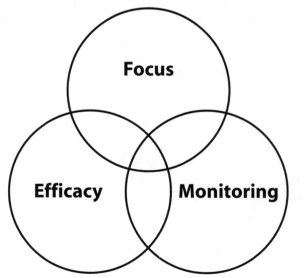

But none of these identified priorities will ever benefit from effective leadership without the confluence of the three essential practices. Our evaluation of 15 leadership practices revealed that a combination of high scores in these three practices—focus, monitoring, and efficacy— yielded strikingly positive results for all schools and all subjects for which we were able to gather student achievement results: reading, writing, math, and science. The power of this combination of leadership practices was consistent, with similar results in the United States and Canada, as well as in student results for high- and low-poverty schools, high- and low-second-language schools, and high- and low-special-needs populations.

Consider the example of formative assessment. There is substantial published research (Hattie, 2009; Marzano, 2009a) that suggests that formative assessment has a positive impact on student achievement. It would be more accurate, however, to say that formative assessment, in the context of a cluster of other related practices, influences achievement. Formative assessment in isolation is no more effective than placing a computer in the classroom and hoping that it will, without software or instruction, improve student results. Formative assessment—accompanied by data analysis, use of the assessment to improve teaching practices, and careful application of those improved teaching practices to student learning—will, in combination, have a strong probability of improving student results. Therefore, it is not a single strategy that improves learning, but rather it is a collection of teaching and leadership practices that, when applied in concert, improve student achievement. It becomes apparent that only by focusing on a limited number of priorities can a school go beyond labels like "formative assessment" to the underlying supportive practices that for that program will produce the desired results.

### The Logic Behind the Focus Imperative

We have already explored the essential nature of focus, and we can infer from the data an informal "rule of six," meaning that schools begin to lose their ability to focus after leaders claim to have more than six priorities. The logic behind the imperative for focus becomes clearer when one considers the other two elements of effective practice, monitoring and efficacy.

## *Monitoring*

Monitoring, in the context of this study, is not merely the collection of data on student performance. Rather, "monitoring" refers to the observation and recording of specific teaching and leadership practices. For example, schools with a commitment to nonfiction writing monitored not only student scores in writing but also the frequency with which teachers in all subjects required nonfiction writing activities from their students. In another illustration, leaders (including administrators and board members) who wished to improve the frequency and quality of classroom observations monitored how many times they visited schools and assessed the clarity and specificity of their visits.

Effective monitoring includes three characteristics. It is frequent, it addresses adult actions, and it is constructive.

### Frequency of Monitoring

First, monitoring must be frequent. Annual monitoring is remarkably ineffective, with data that are late and irrelevant, typically about students who are no longer in class. The impact of frequency is nearly linear, as schools with weekly analysis of student performance and teaching strategies far outdistance schools that monitor only quarterly, semi-annually, or annually (Oberman & Symonds, 2005). The impact of frequent monitoring is directly analogous to the findings reported by Marzano (2007) that frequent monitoring of student performance is directly related to improved achievement. Just a moment ago, the idea of a school having only six priorities might have seemed preposterous—leaders simply must focus on far more than six things. But what if we reconsidered the imperative "focus" in the context of monitoring and created the standard that anything worthy of the label "priority" would require monitoring by the leader at least every week or two? Now, six priorities monitored weekly in a 36-week school year results in 216 discrete instances of monitoring, and the idea of adding a single additional priority with 36 additional instances of monitoring suddenly becomes a daunting task. It is particularly noteworthy that the definitive meta-analysis of leadership practices (Marzano et al., 2005) came to a conclusion that is strikingly similar to ours—higher levels of leadership focus are associated with greater gains in student learning. After an exhaustive review of more than 1,600 studies of the impact of leadership on student achievement, Marzano et al.

identified 21 leadership practices that were associated with immediate and long-term change. Only 3 of the 21 practices met the criteria for both levels of change, and effective monitoring was one of those three.

### Monitoring of Adult Actions

The second characteristic of effective monitoring is that it is focused on adult actions, not merely on student test scores. With modern data collection systems, it may be seductively easy for leaders to claim to engage in monitoring by posting a blizzard of automatically generated charts and graphs of student performance. But if we were monitoring the health of students, surely we would consider more than graphs, however prolifically and elegantly produced, of their weight. We would want to know the causes, not just the effects. If the students lost weight, were they dieting? What were their exercise patterns? What other influences caused them to lose weight? Did they have eating disorders? Were they abusing drugs? These questions would take more time to address, but surely they are at least as important as the simple query of the students' weight.

Similarly, school leaders are now drowning in data (Reeves, 2008–2009), but the data are meaningless unless we consider the causes that lead to the outcomes—that is, the actions of teachers, school leaders, and policymakers. Therefore, a consideration of student achievement results in reading, math, and science must be considered not only as a statement of test scores but also as an assessment of teaching and leadership practices. Monitoring of teachers and school leaders has an unfortunate history—one more likely associated with evaluation, collective bargaining agreements, and job security than with a genuine attempt to improve practice. Nevertheless, there are some outstanding monitoring practices that have been able to coexist with labor agreements (Marshall, 2010). My previous study of leadership evaluation (Reeves, 2009a) suggests that evaluation of leaders suffered from many of the flaws common in teacher evaluation—it was late, it was ineffective, and it tended to regard any behavior above the threshold of felonious assault as "satisfactory." The words "needs improvement" in evaluation should be normal, but in the context of typical monitoring and evaluation systems, the phrase "needs improvement" is a career killer. In the present study, monitoring that was most effective provided frequent and specific feedback to teachers and leaders.

### Constructive Monitoring

The third characteristic of effective monitoring is that it is constructive. Although there are many variations on the walk-through to encourage greater observation of instructional practices in the classroom, all of them can be divided into two broad categories: the witch hunt or the treasure hunt. In the former case, the observer is equipped with a checklist and almost invariably can identify what the teacher is missing. This game of *gotcha!* inspires adversarial relationships and, in many cases in the past decade, has led to the demise of what might otherwise have been promising and thoughtful engagement among teaching professionals. If the price of professional learning and effective feedback is the loss of job security, then we should not expect our colleagues to be enthusiastic participants.

By contrast, even highly unionized school systems have embraced the "science fair" approach to identifying, documenting, and replicating effective practice. Specifically, the science fair (Reeves, 2008a) provides a clear and consistent method for teachers and leaders to document and share professional practices. Connecticut is an international leader in advancing educational accountability by employing methods ranging from a generating a list of test scores through thoughtful, public display of effective professional practices that are directly linked with student achievement. In one recent meeting, more than 400 teams of teachers from throughout the state identified specific data on student achievement, associated the data with measurable professional practices of teachers and administrators, and displayed their findings on three-panel displays in a science fair that brought unanimous acclaim from policymakers, administrators, and union leaders. The guidelines for creating a positive climate for monitoring through a science fair are provided in Appendix D.

## *Efficacy*

The third element of the cluster of professional practices that enhance focus for school leaders is a variable we call "efficacy." In order to understand the power and meaning of the concept of efficacy, try this experiment with your colleagues. Ask a simple, open-ended question: "What are the causes of student achievement?" For the purposes of the study described in this book, the responses to this question were revealed in documents created by teams of administrators and teachers. But the same kind of inquiry can be conducted in any meeting where people are free to speak their mind. By asking the question and noting the responses, you will find that two categories emerge. The first category of responses includes variables that are outside of our control: parental support, nutrition, home language, and so forth. The second category of responses focuses on variables that are within our control: curriculum, assessment, feedback, teaching, leadership, and such. Schools with a high score in efficacy have far more responses in the second category than in the first. These schools operate under the philosophy that, while demographic characteristics of students are certainly important, the actions of teachers and leaders have a greater impact. Either point of view becomes a self-fulfilling prophecy (Reeves, 2006a), a result that is a direct reflection of the pioneering research on the power of expectations documented in *The Pygmalion Effect* (Rosenthal & Jacobson, 2003). More than four decades of research and practice on the power of efficacy leads to the inescapable conclusion that the beliefs of teachers and school leaders have a significant effect, for better or worse, on the performance of students. This power of this variable can be synergistic—magnifying the impact of other teacher influences. Good assessment and curriculum, for example, have greater impacts on student achievement when teachers and administrators have high levels of belief in the effectiveness of those strategies.

## Focus, Monitoring, and Efficacy: The Combined Impact on Performance and Morale

While the imperative for focus is at the heart of this book, the greatest impact on student achievement stems from the combination of this cluster of leadership behaviors. Effective monitoring is possible only when leaders focus on no more than half a dozen instructional leadership priorities. Authentic efficacy is present only if leaders and teachers believe that they have a personal and profound influence on student results. The best news is that the combination of these variables has an impact not only on student performance but also on staff morale. The belief systems of teachers and leaders are directly associated with their levels of stress, anxiety, and burnout (Carbonneau, Vallerand, Fernet, & Guay, 2008). When staff members believe that their efforts are effective for students, their levels of stress, anxiety, and burnout are lower.

This is a strikingly counterintuitive finding. Leaders may think, "I can't ask my staff members to engage in more effective practices—after all, their spouse was just laid off, their neighbor is suffering through a home foreclosure, and their adult children have just moved back into a formerly empty nest." In fact, the opposite is true. Even at a time of personal and economic distress, what staff members need above all is not relief from leadership expectations, but precisely the opposite. Leaders must expect more because it is their expectations that drive efficacy—the belief and reality that the actions of adults do influence student performance. It is imperative that our colleagues know that within the safe harbor of the classroom and the school, our actions still matter, that we do influence results—that we have efficacy.

## CHAPTER 4

# From Theory to Real-World Impact

**I**N THE PREVIOUS CHAPTER I discussed how a few key factors—focus, monitoring, and efficacy—combine to have exceptional impact on student achievement. Let us now turn our attention to research findings and practical applications for school leaders.

## Impact on Student Achievement

While the full details of this study are provided in Appendix A, I list here some of the most striking conclusions about the relationship between focus and student achievement. (Levels of focus discussed here were measured according to the scoring rubric that appears in Appendix B, which is also available for free download at www.tcpress.com and www.LeadandLearn.com.)

- High-poverty schools (those with more than 80% of students categorized as economically disadvantaged) were somewhat more focused than the entire sample, but only 4% of high-poverty schools scored the highest rating on focus, while 30% were at the lowest level. It is no accident that program proliferation affects high-poverty schools, as they receive high levels of funding but invest those funds disproportionately in programs rather than practices.
- Schools with high proportions of second language students rarely showed high levels of focus, with only 2% of schools displaying the highest rating.

- Schools with disproportionately high levels of students eligible for special education services displayed the highest levels of focus, with 5% of schools achieving the highest rating. Unfortunately, 48% of these schools had the lowest level of focus.
- Reading scores were significantly influenced by a combination of high levels of focus and high levels of monitoring. The schools with the highest levels in those two variables achieved twice the gains in reading over 3 years as schools with the lowest levels in the same variables.
- Combinations of variables that excluded focus were inversely related to student achievement. This means that schools that had high scores on the 15-variable scale and were doing precisely as their policymaking jurisdictions required had lower scores in student achievement than did their counterparts that failed to be so compliant. This is a surprising and disturbing finding, so much so that I required our researchers to check the data twice. How could diligence and assiduity be repaid with poor performance? The answer, it turns out, is that without focus, even the most well-intentioned efforts can be counterproductive.
- Leaders must be wary and look behind acronyms. While they can be helpful as mnemonic devices, some of the items that acronyms help us to remember may actually distract from those that are the most important. In fact, acronyms are distinctly unhelpful and uneven in their impact on achievement. Who has not been to a data analysis seminar and heard the exhortation to create "SMART" goals? To my regret, I have parroted this conventional wisdom myself (Reeves, 2002c) and now I must, as researchers are obliged to do, confess error. While "S&M" goals probably will not make the headlines of many professional development conferences, the data reveal that specificity and measurability far outdistance the other elements of the SMART acronym with regard to their impact on student achievement. Indeed, the power of specificity is directly related to the focus variable, and we found that the magnitude of the impact of specificity on student achievement was profound—as much as 10 times greater gains in some subjects when specificity was high compared to when it was low.
- When the relative impact of all variables was evaluated by using factor analysis, focus emerged as having the highest relationship

to student achievement. This finding is entirely consistent with our earlier conclusions. While I am mindful of my own dictum that "life is multivariate," it is also true that some variables are more important than others. Deutchman (2007) concluded that although many complex variables influence healthy weight loss, a few variables such as daily weigh-ins and group support are essential for most individuals. Clearly these practices do not eliminate the need for responsible diet and exercise, but when researchers consider the relative impact of many variables, a few emerge as essential. In the educational context, grading and assessment policies play a similar role. We can have great ideas in curriculum, teaching, and leadership, but without effective grading and assessment policies, even the best practices in curriculum, teaching, and leadership will be undercut (Reeves, 2008b).

Perhaps the best way to conceptualize factor analysis is as a constellation—some people look at the stars and see a random scatter of light; others look at the same stars and see Orion and the Big Dipper. Factor analysis is a technique that allows researchers to think about the relationships among variables in space, like stars in a constellation. Some of the variables tend to form patterns (constellations), or "factor" as the researcher looks at them from different perspectives ("rotations," in the argot of factor analysis). When stars are clustered, a more meaningful relationship is suggested than when they are far apart—we can see the Big Dipper more easily than we can see more diffuse constellations. I acknowledge that factor analysis is properly used as a technique for theory generation and not for the drawing of conclusions (Kim & Mueller, 1978). At the very least, however, it provides a mechanism for understanding the relative relationship between independent variables (in this case, focus) and dependent variables (student achievement).

To this point I have addressed the question of "Why leadership focus?" by providing clear links between improved focus, monitoring, and efficacy and improved achievement. Now I will review each of the leadership practices that were evaluated in this study to measure their impact on student achievement. It was relative to this group of practices that the cluster of three emerged as having the strongest positive relationship to student success.

## Leadership Practices Defined

The following paragraphs define the leadership characteristics that were considered in this study. None of them are without merit, but as we have seen, some are profoundly more influential than others. These leadership practices are defined in a detailed manner in Appendix B, where I also provide a rubric that describes performance of each on three different levels.

It is important to note that I am not offering value judgments about these characteristics. Each of the following sections details laudable goals for educational leaders. Who could possibly be against the leader's establishment of a comprehensive needs analysis or the creation of measurable goals? Any leader would be enthusiastic to commit to each of these objectives. But this enthusiasm is a trap, because the lowest score for each of the following practices results when they are applied with insufficient focus, which is the inevitable result of trying to employ too many programs simultaneously. A leader might make one of these a cornerstone of his or her school, but that adoption would need to be focused, monitored, and invested with a conviction of efficacy in order to be worthwhile.

Not every demand on educational leaders is equal. If we fail to meet the obligation for focus, then the result undermines many other laudable goals, which can be achieved only if leaders are able to distinguish the important from the urgent. When everything is important, then nothing is important. It is therefore no accident that the leaders of school systems with more than a million children score rock bottom in their ability to focus. The paradox is that their competing priorities are neither self-indulgent nor destructive. However, the cumulative effect of multiple priorities is a focus deficit, and the inevitable impact of this deficit is a series of diminishing returns. The following list is not intended to challenge the potential effectiveness of any of the individual practices or characteristics we measured, but it does illustrate the daily conflicts confronted by school leaders. Simply put, when they try to do everything that appears to be effective, the result is that the impact of their frenetic energy is dissipated and student achievement suffers. These practices were selected because we believed when we started the study that all of them have the capacity to highly impact student achievement and we were seeking to discover which ones are most important. Each is described at the implementation level we believe is necessary for success, which is indicative of why too many programs or goals can exhaust a leader and a school.

**EFFICACY**    This variable is based on the attitudes and beliefs of school leaders concerning the causes of student achievement. Efficacy was scored as "high" when leaders indicated that the primary causes of student achievement were effective teaching and leadership, causes within their control. Efficacy was scored as "low" when leaders indicated that the primary causes of student achievement were demographic factors of students, causes beyond their control. The PIM™ research is consistent with findings by other scholars (Marzano, 2003; Rosenthal & Jacobson, 2003) that schools with high efficacy enjoy higher levels of student achievement. Indeed, the PIM™ research so far suggests that schools with the highest efficacy scores experienced more than three times the gains in student achievement over 3 years when compared with schools with the lowest efficacy scores.

**COMPREHENSIVE NEEDS ASSESSMENT**    The comprehensive needs assessment is a tool for broadly assessing a diversity of factors. The process engages staff schoolwide in identifying areas they want to learn more about, organizes study teams to research those areas, and brings information back to the school community as a whole. Essential to this process of discovery, or "treasure hunt," is analysis of "effect variables" in the context of "cause variables." A comprehensive needs assessment includes not only scores but also the strategies for effectiveness, the context, and a description of "antecedents of excellence" that are at the heart of a comprehensive accountability system. Needs assessments are only comprehensive when the data presented describe learning from a variety of meaningful student assessments, and when data about teaching allow the improvement team to examine and identify possible correlations between practice (antecedent conditions, strategies, and structures) and achievement.

**INQUIRY PROCESS**    The inquiry process involves data reduction or prioritization of the information gathered in the previous step. That is, the process invites teams to take the results of their comprehensive needs assessment and identify the "vital few" causes (e.g., two to five cause variables) or professional practices of teachers and leaders (e.g., teaching strategies, assessment practices, feedback techniques, curriculum, monitoring, teacher assignment, etc.) that they believe are significantly related to the school's student achievement shortfalls. Inquiry allows the school improvement team to identify adult actions that contribute to current results and those that are expected to serve as antecedents (predictors) of excellence in the future. Effective inquiry means that teams triangulate available data from the comprehensive needs assessment to identify existing correlations of cause and effect and generate questions for which answers are desirable but unavailable from current data. These two sources of evidence and ideas serve as a basis for prioritization of needs and development of hypotheses for action. Inquiry is not complete unless prioritized hypotheses are developed.

**SPECIFIC GOALS**   Goals will have both broad-based and long-term impact because they are focused on the specific content needs of the specific students for whom each goal is intended.

**MEASURABLE GOALS**   Goals are structured in such a way that it is possible to know whether school improvement actions are resulting in the kind of difference desired. Measurable goals simply describe quantifiable results to allow determination of the degree of their impact or influence. Therefore, establishing clear baseline data is critical to measuring a change in results from current reality to preferred reality (goal). Measurement can and should occur in a number of different ways using a variety of different tools and strategies (e.g., large-scale and school-based measures). Seeing results across measurements that yield consistent patterns gives greater confidence that school improvement actions truly have made a difference.

**ACHIEVABLE (ATTAINABLE) GOALS**   The goal statement is within the realm of the leader's influence or control and was developed based on current student achievement levels, capacity of staff, and available resources. Additionally, attainment of achievable goals will always narrow the achievement gaps present in the lowest performing student subgroups and will eliminate them altogether within a 3–5-year period.

**RELEVANT GOALS** Goals reflect the urgent, critical needs previously identified through the school's inquiry process and align well with the district's strategic targets. Goals are clearly selected as a result of a careful needs analysis (e.g., comprehensive needs analysis and inquiry process).

**TIMELY GOALS** Each of the goals identifies specific dates for assessment and data collection and analysis. The chosen dates occur at appropriately frequent intervals (e.g., criterion- and norm-referenced tests occur yearly; teacher-created, classroom-level, or common assessments occur monthly; others quarterly; etc.). Further, there is a clear rationale behind the established timeline for goal assessment; it is neither formulaic nor random.

**TARGETED RESEARCH-BASED STRATEGIES** Every strategy selected should be informed by sound research on effective teaching strategies and school practices and by other standards-based initiatives (e.g., classroom walk-throughs, data walls, data teams, instructional or assessment calendars, posting of standards, Marzano's *The Art and Science of Teaching* [2007], Northwest Regional Educational Laboratory [NWREL] and other standards-based initiatives, etc.). Additionally, the practices the school adopts should directly impact classroom instructional practices and should be designed to reshape administrative structures to support improved instruction. Finally, for these strategies to be truly effective, they need to be targeted to the student subgroups most in need of their application. For instance, if Individualized Education Plan (IEP) students with learning disabilities struggle with short-term memory and vocabulary (as most do), then it is wise to select strategies that help students activate prior knowledge and retain and apply that knowledge as well. Nonlinguistic representations, structured use of advanced organizers and questioning cues, and extra time and opportunity to practice application of rich vocabulary terms at grade-level standard are examples of such strategies.

**MASTER PLAN DESIGN** The master plan design is a concise blueprint of the action steps or Tier 2 indicators (which consistently describe how strategies will be implemented) that will allow anyone in the school to understand the adult practices, which will be regularly measured and monitored to ensure effective implementation. Additionally, the master plan provides evidence of midcourse correction opportunities (e.g., continuous improvement cycles, plan–do–study–act cycles) and demonstrates a capacity for rapid team responses and support when adjustments are warranted. The timelines outlined must be realistic, clear, and specific for each action step. Each action step should designate an appropriate "entity responsible"—an individual who coordinates implementation of that action step. The action steps and timelines for each goal and strategy should be systematic and coordinated with each other.

**PROFESSIONAL DEVELOPMENT EMPHASIS**    The professional development identified within the plan is designed to be sustained over time, clearly aligns with each school goal, and is associated with a limited number of professional development strategies explicitly linked to the school goals. Professional development activities maintain a schoolwide focus. Teachers learn new instructional strategies, and the plan outlines how administrators will supervise, support, and evaluate teachers in light of these new strategies. In a majority of professional development action steps, consideration of adult learning needs and change processes is clearly evident and reflected in time, strategies, and resources (e.g., limited initiatives, aligned and focused professional development, integrated planning, related support structures, etc.) to sustain growth over time.

**PROFESSIONAL DEVELOPMENT IMPLEMENTATION**    All key program implementation action steps contained within the plan are supported by specific research-based professional development strategies. Timelines for professional development are well thought out. That is, complex strategies have a long and cyclical period for learning, whereas simpler ones rely on a shorter timeline. A good match exists between the professional development plans outlined and the resources allocated to accomplish them.

**PARENTAL INVOLVEMENT STRATEGIES**    The school improvement plan should specify creative and empowering ways to include parents in the important work of improving student achievement. The plan should identify areas where parents might need further training and education, and describe how that training will be provided. The plan should incorporate parent-friendly communication practices (in the primary language of the parent; scheduled during day, evening, and weekend times; in settings that are comfortable and professional) to engage parents with report cards, newsletters, progress reports, phone call practices, and conferences. The emphasis is on involvement that improves student achievement rather than requiring onsite participation, and there is a conscious inclusion of parental involvement in the school improvement plan's action steps. Traditional strategies that contribute to improved student achievement include serving on committees, tutoring, assisting in classrooms, or targeted fund-raising for new literature books or instructional materials.

**MONITORING PLAN** The monitoring plan describes—for a majority of school improvement goals—explicit data to be monitored, when they will be monitored, and who will be responsible for reporting progress. A continuous improvement cycle is evident in the monitoring plan, describing opportunities to alter the plan and make midcourse adjustments. The plan clearly articulates the type of data to be collected and analyzed. Specifically, monitoring of student achievement covers a range of assessment data (e.g., annual assessments, quarterly benchmarks, monthly probes, common formative assessments) that are specified in the school improvement plan. The plan also provides for monitoring of improved teaching practices (degree of implementation, percentage of teachers collaborating, number of teachers posting data) and distributes monitoring responsibility across a range of individuals who will conduct data collection and analysis.

**MONITORING FREQUENCY** The plan specifies the frequency of monitoring progress toward achievement of goals. Specifically, the school improvement plan provides for frequent monitoring of student achievement (5–10 times annually). Furthermore, the monitoring schedules assist the school in reviewing teaching practices as well as student performance. The timeline describes explicit dates or weeks in which each monitoring activity will occur. The plan relies on these monitoring junctures to support decisions, rather than unrealistically assuming that constant (daily or ongoing) monitoring will be conducted. Monitoring responsibility is distributed across a range of individuals so that monitoring can occur frequently enough to identify problems as they occur.

**EVALUATION CYCLE**   The evaluation plan allows the school to compare planned with achieved outcomes. Specifically, the plan describes how compared results (positive and negative) will be communicated to primary stakeholders (families, educators, staff, patrons, partners, and the public) and how lessons learned will be applied to future school improvement planning, implementation, and monitoring cycles. The evaluation portion of the plan is part of a continuous improvement plan timeline. A yearlong calendar identifies specific, coordinated dates for each of the elements of the improvement cycle for *all* goals. The plan explicitly describes the actions that will be taken in light of the outcome data.

## Lead Like a Lifeguard

Achieving focus is possible only if we are able to set some clear and specific priorities. Like lifeguards, school leaders are faced with many potential distractions and competing priorities, and much is at stake for those in their charge if they do not keep their attention on what is most important. At the end of the day, their performance will be judged by their effectiveness in achieving their objectives and avoiding disaster. The lifeguard is never credited for the potential drownings his vigilance prevented; he is only recognized for the dramatic rescues that land him in the news. Similarly, the educational leader is not recognized for the potential failures that his focus and planning prevented. But the evidence presented in this volume suggests that it is the leadership decisions that are made not in the drama of the moment but in the quiet anticipation of disaster that have the greatest impact on the lives of students and their communities.

## CHAPTER 5

# Weeding the Garden

**F**OCUS IS EASY TO TALK ABOUT and difficult to implement. Educators and administrators who applaud an emphasis on focus and nod knowingly at the Law of Initiative Fatigue suddenly disengage when the question is put to them, "What will you give up?" The most common answer is, "Nothing—everything that I do is important. It's other people—national governments, provincial ministries, state departments, superintendents, principals, department heads—who are responsible for the wasted time."

In this chapter, I will explore practical procedures for identifying specific things that leaders can take off the table. It is difficult to overstate how important this step is. Too frequently, the term "focus" is used as a synonym for "emphasis"—as in "I expect you to focus on monitoring effective teaching practices, but I'm not going to relieve you of any other requirements, so you won't have any extra time, energy, or resources to really do what I am asking you to focus on." Leadership focus depends, therefore, not only on identifying those leadership practices that are effective—specific and measurable goals, monitoring of teaching and leadership practices, and feedback for students that is accurate and timely—but also on clearly articulating what we will not do. This process is similar to weeding a garden, and it is difficult for similar reasons: One person's dandelion is another person's orchid. Nevertheless, it is important to identify weeds in our schools and eliminate them, and it is dangerous if we fail.

*The New Oxford American Dictionary* (McKean, 2005) defines a weed as "a wild plant growing where it is not wanted and in competition with cultivated plants." This definition captures the essence of why this analogy is so important in a consideration of leadership focus. It is not just that weeds are unsightly, undesirable, and noxious. It is that their very presence competes for resources—nutrients, water, and space—with the food we are growing to nourish our bodies and the roses that nurture our souls.

I will describe three primary categories of "weeds" that hinder school progress. The first type is diversionary weeds—they steal nutrients from the soil. Then there are weeds that can spread toxic pathogens that infect the flowers around them, or others that smother the flowers by stealing their light and air. And some weeds are plants that might be appropriate in one environment, but when they are introduced into the wrong environment, they create nonsustainable conditions. Finally, I will address the nature of weed eradication—the specific actions by educational leaders that are necessary in order to identify, remove, and avoid weeds.

## Diversionary Weeds

Weeds are not evil intruders. They do what all biological systems do by growing, reproducing, and evolving. Whatever one's opinion of Charles Darwin and his theories may be, we at least owe it to him on the bicentennial of his birth to quote him accurately. Biological evolution is not about the "survival of the fittest," but rather about adaptation. In Darwin's words, "It is not the strongest of the species that survives, nor the most intelligent that survives. It is the one that is the most adaptable to change."

When resources are abundant, weeds can prosper alongside native species, and the species that are cultivated can support human needs. But in a finite world, the success of one plant means the starvation of another. In educational systems, as in biological ones, weeds grow, reproduce, and adapt to their environment, diverting resources of time, money, and emotional energy from other needs.

Diversionary weeds often begin as a benign presence. They take the form of a well-intended announcement or earnest "sharing" of information in a faculty meeting designed for professional learning. Or perhaps it is a willingness by the school board to hear public comments at the beginning of a meeting that was to have been devoted to deep inquiry into the board's commitment to student achievement. In neither case were the intrusions the result of ill intent, but in both cases the introduction of a weed robbed the educators, leaders, and policymakers of time that can never be recovered.

Once the diversionary weeds have staked a claim on a portion of the garden, they spread with alarming speed. The momentary announcement becomes a laundry list, robbing precious minutes from professional learning opportunities. The public comment period in a board meeting—seemingly the bedrock of democracy—becomes a complaint-fest for malcontents and has counterproductive effects, preventing the board from doing what they were elected to do. While faculty meetings are typically governed by the clock and bargaining agreements, board meetings are governed only by the endurance of the majority. But the elasticity of time is an illusion, because the agenda items considered at 11:00 p.m. never receive the time and attention of those considered 3 hours earlier, when the meeting began.

What makes diversionary weeds so difficult to control is their earnest intent and good appearance. The Melaleuca plant is tended, nourished, and advertised in some nations, while it is a weed in other nations. Similarly, simple and inoffensive practices such as announcements and public comment are prized in some environments, such as Athenian democracy, but are unhelpful when the objective of a group is to focus on professional learning or public policy-making. Demosthenes, the greatest orator of ancient Greece, honed his craft according to legend by reciting orations with rocks in his mouth. Equipped with rhetorical skill, he inspired his fellow Athenians into battle against arch-rival Sparta. But as any reliable Spartan will testify, when the people heard Demosthenes, they said, "How well he spoke." But when Demosthenes's rival addressed the crowds, the people said, "Let us march." Rhetorical weeds—the stuff of the inspirational speeches that open every school year—remind us that actions speak louder than words. The planners of these dreadful events say, "How well he spoke," while the teachers in the dark auditoriums say, "Let us march."

This is precisely the comparison that educational leaders should make when considering the intrusion of potentially diversionary weeds into the school day, professional learning meeting, or board agenda. If we imagine the best conceivable outcome as the one Demosthenes received—people are impressed with the words—then it is a weed. It is an elegant, rhetorical, pleasant weed to be sure. But it is a weed nevertheless. If, on the other hand, the intrusion compels us to action, then it deserves more careful consideration. Guskey (2000) has done a superb job of helping educational leaders distinguish pleasing rhetoric from essential impact. His five levels of professional development have application far beyond the workshop. If we consider the continuum from pleasing presentation (Level 1) to impact on student achievement (Level 5), then we have a blueprint for creating boundaries around every educational activity, from the classroom to the boardroom.

The practical considerations regarding how to identify and eliminate diversionary weeds are clear and significant. Because we acknowledge that these weeds can have value in other contexts, it is not necessary to kill them, but only to move them to a different environment. Announcements and well-intended sharing by faculty members do not need to be eliminated, but they can be transferred from a professional development forum to a website, bulletin board, or other format that does not compete for time and attention with professional learning. Public commentary is certainly at the heart of democracy, but it does not have to rob board meetings of time and focus. Effective boards can distinguish opportunities for public hearings—perhaps chaired by one or two board members in geographically diverse contexts—from public deliberations, which are focused on inquiry, learning, and decision-making by elected officials.

## Toxic Weeds

There is an important exception to my previous claim that weeds do not have personalities: Canadian thistles are pure evil. They emit a painful sting. They grow in a maniacal subterranean network. They strangle their neighbors, wrapping their tentacles around them like an octopus on land. And they might be members of your faculty, cabinet, or board. Toxic weeds demand a response, and in too many organizational settings, we are reluctant to challenge and remove them. The reason for this reluctance is a perverse logic that elevates the appearance of competence over the best interests of the organization. After all, Canadian thistles are very, very good at what they do. Similarly, toxic weeds in school systems are undeniably effective. They represent people, programs, and practices that are seductive in their apparent competence. They look good, they sound good, and they can even make people feel good, at least in the short term. But once these weeds are introduced into the environment, they strangle the life out of the other plants that we had hoped to cultivate.

Toxic weeds manifest themselves in behaviors and programs. Behavioral toxic weeds have been best described as "competent jerks" (Casciaro & Lobo, 2005). These are people who dominate meetings and public forums with their conclusions, assessments, and judgments, some of which are based upon facts—that is what makes them competent. But some of their conclusions, assessments, and judgments are gratuitous and cruel. A colleague, in the expressed view of this toxic member, does not make a mistake, but is labeled by the critic as stupid. A chart does not have a mislabeled axis, but is a deliberate misrepresentation. A policy is not misinformed, but is malicious. The difference between a rational critic and a jerk is that the former focuses on the policy or the error that needs to be addressed, and the latter focuses negatively on the person.

When considering the impact of toxic weeds, we should think in terms of not only the competent jerk but also the supremely competent spider. I wept through readings of *Charlotte's Web* (by E. B. White) with four children, but after receiving a spider bite in Cuba, my sympathy for arachnids disappeared. A simple red spot turns into a large 10-inch black-and-blue region that then descends into muscle and tissue. A little venom—the insult, challenge to integrity, rumor, and innuendo—can cause damage that is serious and long-lasting.

## Unsustainable Programmatic Weeds

Some weeds are fine when we limit their ability to spread—that is, when they exist in small numbers, they are not offensive to the eye or to neighboring species, but when they proliferate, they may take over the environment so aggressively that even their own offspring are not able to survive. Some species of pine trees fall into this category and thus are regarded by plant scientists as weeds.

Just as it is odd to think of a pine tree as a weed, so also is it challenging to label what would otherwise be a fine idea for curriculum, professional development, leadership, or assessment as a weed. But no matter how meritorious an idea might be in isolation, it becomes a weed when it is unsustainable.

Consider the example of formative assessment. Certainly the evidence is overwhelming that formative assessment is essential as a mechanism for providing effective feedback to students and teachers (Ainsworth & Viegut, 2006; Popham, 2008; Wiggins, 1998). In some schools, frequent formative assessments are provided, with students and teachers receiving feedback the same day, and teachers using the data to improve instruction the next day. But while formative assessment done well is a rose in the educational garden, too many formative assessment systems have become uncontrollable weeds. It is only a short step from good intention to chaos. Vendors offer test banks with thousands of items, helpfully linked to key words which, they claim, will assist teachers in finding test items related to each standard. Teachers are required to provide evidence that students are proficient on each standard, and they recall from a college assessment class that they should have six items for each standard they wish to assess. Soon the computer has generated assessments that include more than 80 items and require more than 2 hours for students to complete. The reports, elegant and detailed to be sure, remain in the district assessment office, and are delivered to the teachers and principals long after the information might have been used to inform instruction.

In these unsustainable systems, teachers and administrators either stop administering the assessments or provide glum compliance with administration of the tests but never use them in a formative manner. Worse yet, the time consumed by unsustainable programs robs classrooms of time and energy that would be better devoted to improved teaching and learning.

## Eradicating Weeds

Removing the appearance of weeds by taking the tops off of them does nothing to improve the health of a garden. Roots are deep and the weeds continue to spread, choking the life out of neighboring plants. Similarly, removing the appearance of curriculum weeds—for example, by the publication of a new, streamlined curriculum—will have little impact if the new curriculum is not associated with instructional observations and meaningful assessments. Changing the agenda of a staff meeting or board meeting will have no lasting impact if leaders continue to tolerate interruptions, announcements, and commentary that are beyond the scope of the meeting. It is not just the removal of the weeds that is necessary, but continued monitoring, observation, and weeding that keeps the garden healthy.

Toxic weeds such as Canadian thistle are remarkably resistant to the efforts of even the most diligent gardener. Grab them with your hands and suffer a dozen painful barbs; grab them with gloves and the barbs can go right through them. Try to poison them and you risk damaging the vegetables and flowers occupying the same ground, and even the most aggressive chemicals sometimes fail to deter the persistent thistle. I have seen gardeners give up on eradication and bring in tons of new dirt in order to establish a bed of fresh, weed-free soil.

Sometimes, schools can make remarkable turnarounds with minimal changes in staff, provided that leadership is strong and consistent in support of effective practices. Val Verde Unified School District in California provides a remarkable example of effective reform that did not entail a complete reconstitution of the school (Reeves, 2007). While dramatically increasing student achievement in this high-poverty, high-minority, and high-second-language school, only a few teachers left. The essential change was in the professional practices of teachers, not in the personnel in the schools. The teachers devoted more time to literacy, established a commitment to student achievement that was consistent and relentless, and agreed to a dramatically revised set of consequences for poor student performances. Rather than punishing students with grades of F or zero, the teachers became relentless in their demands for proficient work.

In other cases, however, the practices that inhibit achievement have become so deeply embedded that the only solution is reconstitution. Manual High School, once a showcase of urban high school success in Denver, suffered from chronic low achievement, high dropout rates, and poor faculty morale. After several unsuccessful interventions, the school was closed and reconstituted with a completely new vision for student success (*Denver Post*, June 13, 2007).

While the Colorado reconstitution appears promising, the results elsewhere have been mixed, particularly when the changes in the school are superficial and there are no changes to address underlying systemic problems that influence student achievement. For example, interviews with leaders in one Texas district where two schools were reconstituted revealed that because the district maintained staffing seniority policies that continued to fill the highest-poverty schools with the least-experienced teachers and administrators, it failed to make fundamental reforms in assessment and teaching. Worse yet, the system attempted to address its instructional deficiencies with a raft of new programs and a dizzying array of required training, most of which involved introductory material but lacked depth and application. Precisely when these schools needed more focus, they received more initiatives. When they needed to nurture a few flowers, they scattered their attention.

Now that I have explored the research behind the imperative for focus and exhausted the metaphor of the weeds, I will move on to a consideration of how systems and schools establish and maintain leadership focus. This is not a singular event, but a continuous process. Leaders who are committed to focus are relentless, not only when they initially remove distractions from their greatest priorities, but on a daily basis. They routinely challenge interruptions that creep into their days in the form of e-mails, meetings, and tasks that fail to answer their essential questions of relevance, purpose, and impact.

## CHAPTER 6

# Focus at the System Level

THE COMPELLING CONCLUSION of the research is that schools with higher levels of focus not only have higher levels of student achievement but also are better able to implement other essential leadership and teaching strategies. In many cases, school leaders fall victim to the Law of Initiative Fatigue involuntarily, because their scattershot approach to programs reflects a similarly diffused and growing set of requirements from higher authorities. Therefore, in order for schools to focus, it is necessary first to address mechanisms to help the entire school system establish leadership focus.

Fortunately, there is evidence not only in this study but elsewhere that this is possible. Levin (2008) documents in a convincing manner the case of Ontario, where the Ministry of Education created widespread systemic improvements for more than 5,000 schools as they established a focus on literacy, numeracy, and decisive intervention for students in need. Fullan (2005, 2008a), Hargreaves and Fink (2006), and Hargreaves and Fullan (2009) have similarly documented cases across different cultures and governance structures of sustainable change, and focus is invariably an element of that success.

Because systems tend to be hierarchical in nature, the impact of their decisions resembles a pyramid, with a few decisions at the top leading to a multiplicity of mandates, initiatives, and priorities at the bottom. In a system committed to focus, by contrast, the shape changes dramatically, from a pyramid to a diamond. For example, most traditional educational organizations are a hierarchical pyramid, with an administrator at the top, and lower ranking administrators at the bottom. In a typical pyramid organization, there is a point at the top—the leader—and from that point all orders and communications descend to the lower levels of the pyramid, where leadership commands are executed. Envision, by contrast, a glistening diamond and think about what you notice, looking from the inside out. The facets of the diamond connect each part of the gem to the others along a seemingly infinite variety of pathways. Sunlight enters not only from the "top" down, but at any point on the face of the stone. In the diamond organization, innovations arise from throughout the organization, not just from initiatives announced from the top. Communication in the diamond organization travels in every direction, not just from the top and directed downward. The brilliance of the diamond depends not upon the impressiveness of one part of the stone, but upon the ability of each part, wherever it may be, to refract the light and dazzle the observer. Certainly there are times when the pyramid organization works and the principles of "command and control" are necessary, such as when evacuating a burning building. But if you want the same people to generate exceptional levels of creativity and the communication essential for a 21st-century organization, the diamond is a superior model. Consider the popular computer operating system, Linux, which was developed using a network, not a traditional hierarchy. The fact that IBM, one of the most famously hierarchical organizations in the world, now uses Linux illustrates that hierarchy and networks can coexist.

Although schools and other governmental entities are by nature hierarchical, they need not maintain the toxic elements of hierarchy that create confusion, harm relationships, and diminish impact (Hamel, 2009). In fact, networks can function within a hierarchy, and the use of networks allows communication channels to expand while the system maintains and refines its focus.

## Two Essential Questions

Leaders must ask two essential questions about every decision they consider. First, "What is the extent of my ability to influence this action?" Second, "What impact will this action have on the student learning results I am seeking to achieve?" However obvious these two questions may be, it is astonishing how much leadership time, how many agenda items, and how much professional learning time is spent on matters that fail the test raised by these two questions.

Try this simple experiment. Consider the agenda—both the written one and the list of matters that were actually discussed—of a recent faculty meeting, cabinet meeting, or board meeting. In Figure 6.1, list 10 topics that you can recall and rate each one of them for leadership influence and impact on results on a scale of 1 to 10, with 10 representing the highest level of influence or impact. For example, if the agenda item you consider is opposition by a taxpayer advocacy group to a proposed bond issue, your ability to influence the matter—persuading the group to endorse the bond issue—may be a "1" but the impact it has on your results may be a "10." A discussion of faculty parking spaces may be a "10" in terms of the leader's ability to influence it, but chances are that the impact on results is near zero. Complete Figure 6.1 now.

**FIGURE 6.1**   Influence and Impact

| Agenda Items | Leadership Influence (1–10) | Impact on Results (1–10) |
|---|---|---|
|  |  |  |
|  |  |  |
|  |  |  |
|  |  |  |
|  |  |  |
|  |  |  |
|  |  |  |
|  |  |  |
|  |  |  |
|  |  |  |

This figure is available for free download and printing from www.tcpress.com.

As you evaluate each agenda item, consider which allows you to respond affirmatively to the two essential questions. As you recall the agenda item and the various levels of satisfaction or frustration that these memories elicit, four different categories of potential leadership actions become clear. Potential actions with low influence and low results are exercises in futility. These are the perhaps cathartic but ultimately point-less discussions in faculty meetings about "kids these days" that do not lead to any meaningful change either in the students or in the way we engage with them.

Actions with high influence and low results are the stuff of bureau-cratic imperialism. I have witnessed school boards debate the color of tile in a high school cafeteria and have seen superintendents personally take charge of ordering equipment for the weight room. One need only look at the vendor displays at national conventions of board members and superintendents to realize that marketers are well aware that policy-makers and very senior leaders get involved in a wide array of supply purchases that are within their authority to make but are far removed from any relationship to what those leaders and policymakers would claim are their top priorities.

Actions with low influence and high impact on results offer potential for enormous frustration. We know, for example, that attendance of students has a dramatic impact on our results, yet there are often factors that inhibit attendance that are beyond the control of leaders. Collective bargaining agreements, the international economy and accompanying job loss in the community, and a series of environmental factors have a high impact on schools, but are often beyond the control of leaders.

Finally, there are actions that are at the intersection of high influence and high impact, and it is in this quadrant where focused leaders spend the vast majority of their time. Figure 6.2 illustrates this leadership focus matrix. If a potential action is within your authority but has low impact, it does not belong on the leader's desk and should be dropped. If the task has high potential impact but the leader lacks authority, then there may be opportunities to negotiate greater authority.

For the 75% of this matrix that harms the ability of leaders to focus, there are only two alternatives. First, we can increase the influence of the leader. For example, while the issue of student attendance may initially appear to be outside the control of the leader, there is research to suggest that decisions over which leaders exercise a great deal of control can have a significant and immediate impact on student attendance (Reeves,

**FIGURE 6.2**   Leadership Focus Matrix

| | Low | Personal Authority | High |
|---|---|---|---|
| **High** Impact | High Impact, Low Authority<br><br>**NEGOTIATE IT** | | High Impact, High Authority<br><br>**DO IT!** |
| **Low** | Low Impact, Low Authority<br><br>**AVOID IT** | | Low Impact, High Authority<br><br>**DROP IT** |

2008c). Erickson (2010) described how specific changes in school policy led to a 42% improvement in unexcused absences at a Minnesota middle school. Specifically, the school disconnected attendance from grading. In the past, when students had an unexcused absence, the consequence was an F for the day and students were prohibited from making up the classwork or tests for that day. But despite this consequence, unexcused absences continued. Erickson and his colleagues changed the consequences for unexcused absences from poor grades to a combination of parental notification and personal discussions with students. Although many skeptics predicted that disconnecting grades from attendance would lead to skyrocketing attendance problems, the results established the opposite. Students were not influenced by poor grades as a punishment, but their behavior changed remarkably when they were faced with parental notification and personal contacts with school officials.

Second, we can increase the impact of the decision on results. For example, some policies may have potential impact but are inadequately monitored. The most common example here is the use of data for improved instructional decisions. A study by the Association of California School Administrators (ACSA) demonstrated that when schools conducted data analysis linking student performance and teaching practices more frequently, they had better results. Simply making the data available was not enough; leaders needed to monitor the frequency and effectiveness with which the data were used. The evidence from this study strongly suggests that when monitoring is combined with other leadership actions, the leverage is very high. School plans that are nearly identical in every respect—specific and measurable goals, targeted professional development, clear data analyses—may have high or low impact based on the degree of monitoring associated with them. Therefore, what may appear to be a low-impact leadership action may not necessarily need to be changed or avoided; perhaps it simply needs to be monitored. This is particularly true when it comes to matters of curriculum, assessment, and feedback. Improvements in these areas are illusory if implementation involves little more than the delivery of three-ring binders to schools and pro forma workshops to teachers. When, by contrast, leadership monitoring improves, the impact of assessment, curriculum, and feedback improvements can be dramatic. Ben Davis High school, located near the Indianapolis Airport, reduced their failure rate by more than 1,000 courses in a single year (Reeves, 2006b) under a coordinated program accompanied by careful monitoring. The techniques used were not new. Specifically, seven practices were employed:

1. Early, frequent, and decisive intervention.
2. Personal connection with struggling students.
3. Parent connections.
4. Tutoring by teachers, peer tutors, and "study buddies" who provide students with one-to-one assistance.
5. Managing students' choices with decisive curriculum interventions.
6. In-school assistance.
7. Reformed grading systems.

None of these seven practices would have been successful as an isolated program. The key was leadership focus.

## Toward Multidimensional Perspectives of Leadership

Although a commitment to leadership has an undeniable impact on the effectiveness and efficiency of an organization, that commitment is necessary but not sufficient to sustain improvements in leadership. Figure 6.3 describes the most common areas of focus for leadership develop-

**FIGURE 6.3**   Two-Dimensional Perspective

| | Personal | Organizational |
|---|---|---|
| **Performance** | Goal is *Efficiency*: Achieve personal objectives and manage time, projects, and people | Goal is *Effectiveness*: Achieve organizational goals and execute coordinated strategies |
| **Therapeutic** | Goal is *Satisfaction*: Achieve sense of personal approval and reassurance | Goal is *Comfort*: Achieve cooperation and conflict resolution |

ment (Reeves, 2009a; Reeves & Allison, 2009). The horizontal axis represents the target of a proposed change—either an individual leader or the entire organization. The vertical axis represents whether the proposed leadership change is therapeutic, addressing behavior and emotions of the leader, or related to performance, such as analysis, communication, and teamwork.

The resulting combination of factors yields four strikingly different conceptions of change. A great deal of professional development for leaders takes place at the intersection of the personal and therapeutic dimensions, defining success as individual satisfaction. If the leader is happy, then the program was a success. This sort of intervention is often focused on leaders who are struggling with high levels of stress, anxiety, and personal challenges. At the intersection of the personal and performance dimensions is the quadrant focused on efficiency. These improvement efforts are typically associated with the leader's time, project, and task management. Success means doing tasks more quickly and efficiently. At the intersection of the organizational and therapeutic dimensions the goal is the emotional comfort of leaders and staff members, and the work here is often associated with conflict resolution and dealing with high levels of organizational stress. At the intersection of the organizational and performance dimensions is a focus on effectiveness and the execution of organizational strategies.

There is certainly nothing wrong with any of these quadrants. Who could possibly be against personal and organizational improvement? Who doesn't want more efficiency and effectiveness? The central challenge for system-level focus is that each of these quadrants can lead to a growing list of demands, each of which is, in isolation, a fine idea. Nevertheless, their cumulative effect is to elevate the levels of stress, anxiety, and burnout that they were intended to relieve. Take a closer look at Figure 6.3, and imagine that you are attempting to focus on the intersection of the therapeutic and the personal—at the same time you are pushing to address issues in the other three quadrants. It is easy to see how burnout could be the end result.

What could go wrong with diligent efforts in the lower right-hand quadrant, where the focus is on conflict resolution? Certainly many organizations would benefit from a commitment to civil discourse and addressing conflict in a thoughtful and constructive manner. But conflict management by itself is an inappropriate goal for any organization that aspires to grow, change, and improve. Change by its very nature implies conflict, because it necessitates letting go of previous practices, attitudes, and beliefs. Indeed, one of the leader's primary responsibilities is not to control or manage conflict, but to ensure that inevitable conflict is about, in Fullan's wonderful turn of phrase, "what's worth fighting for" (Fullan, 2008b). The late John Kenneth Galbraith, one of the leading voices of social reform in the 20th century, suggested to the many Presidents he counseled that they should seek to "comfort the afflicted [and] afflict the comfortable." This is not bad advice for leaders whose goal is not stasis—as if that were ever a possible choice—but rather who recognize that improvement and inevitable change of necessity mean discomfort. Although many people have heard that successful leadership change requires prior buy-in before change can be implemented, that presumption does not square with the evidence. In fact, it is essential that leaders act "as if" they had the assent of their colleagues (Fullan, 2010) while implementing change. The temptation to wait for universal buy-in is a prescription for paralysis. In fact, it is not necessary to resolve every conflict. On the contrary, if conflict is not present, then it is very likely that the change is not significant.

The upper right quadrant addresses the execution of effective strategies, the subject of innumerable business journal articles and books. What else is there besides organizational effectiveness? Isn't that enough? First, the entire notion of strategic planning, particularly in the context of education, must be subjected to serious scrutiny (Reeves, 2002a; Schmoker, 2004). Too much of what is called strategy is the creation of planning documents rather than leadership *actions* that will have a direct impact on organizational goals. There is a deeper reason why all of these quadrants are not sustainable simultaneously, and that is that each one's internal focus is exclusively on the needs of the organization or of the individuals within it.

## Beyond Efficiency and Effectiveness: The Power of the Greater Good

What would happen if we were to add a third dimension to the scale, reflecting an external focus on the greater good? Researchers Noémie Carbonneau and colleagues (2008) reference "harmonious passion" to describe the level of engagement of educators who not only care deeply about what they are accomplishing but also perceive that they are capable of influencing the result. Daniel Pink (2009) offers a thoughtful survey of the research on human motivation and performance, which suggests that meaningful work is at the heart of human motivation. Theresa Amabile and Steven Kramer (2010) find that humans need a purpose beyond work to achieve real motivation. This multidimensional perspective would suggest that my happiness is insufficient unless I am considering the happiness of others; my efficiency and effectiveness represent not success but self-absorption unless I also take the needs of others into account. Figure 6.4 illustrates this challenge, with the star in the upper right-hand portion of the diagram signifying that the four basic quadrants are not sufficient if we lack resilience, the ability to respond to adversity—and renewal, a source of recurring energy that emanates not from self-satisfaction but from contribution.

Think of people you know who represent the four quadrants. Starting in the upper left-hand quadrant, some friends are efficient. They are regularly at the gym, never display a trace of organizational conflict, and have strategies that would be the envy of the D-Day planners. But their focus on performance alone does not give them much comfort; in fact, they can be miserable. Consider people who are about to enjoy great music or theater but ruin the experience for themselves and others as

**FIGURE 6.4**  Multidimensional Perspective for the Greater Good

## Sustained Change
### Focus on the Greater Good

| | Personal | Organizational |
|---|---|---|
| **Performance** | **The Essential Intersection**: Sustained personal and organizational performance | |
| | Goal is *Efficiency*: Achieve personal objectives and manage time, projects, and people | Goal is *Effectiveness*: Achieve organizational goals and execute coordinated strategies |
| **Therapeutic** | Goal is *Satisfaction*: Achieve sense of personal approval and reassurance | Goal is *Comfort*: Achieve cooperation and conflict resolution |

Resilience · Renewal

they pursue relentlessly improved efficiency and effectiveness—typically as they tap their digital devices during the most sublime moments of a concert. In their zeal for efficiency, they have forsaken the pursuit of beauty and rest.

Leaders need to focus on the common good—not just on efficiency and effectiveness.

Carbonneau et al. (2008) distinguish harmonious passion from "obsessive passion," describing the former as stemming from intrinsic motivations and willing actions, while the latter uses the education profession merely as a psychological tool. The goal in obsessive passion is not the greater good, but merely the illusion of public service to improve one's personal sense of worth. Harmonious passion is not antithetical to efficiency and effectiveness, but it is distinctive in two ways. First, it represents passion about things we can control. Improving the literacy skills of students can, to a large degree, be influenced by the passion and diligence of teachers. And this particular passion is also about something that is deeply important, providing a lifetime of improved opportunity for students. Because we can influence the outcome and the goal is important, this sort of passion is harmonious. By contrast, passion invested in things we cannot control—such as the home language or the family structure of our students—is disharmonious. While much of the focus of improving student results is measured by improvement in scores, our colleagues are less likely to invest their passion in producing a 5% gain in scores than they are to find passion in the *meaning* of improved student results—the lifetime of happiness and success those students will find possible with improved education and that will be impossible without essential literacy skills.

## From the Pyramid to the Diamond

Organizations are almost always hierarchies. Boards have chairpersons; school systems have superintendents and directors. Almost all institutions, from international religious organizations to governmental entities, have clearly designated leaders. Similarly, local schools almost always use some sort of hierarchical organization to get things done. The exceptions can be interesting sources for study, as some schools have demonstrated that nonhierarchical student and teacher leadership can be remarkably effective and, in fact, can help students prepare to assume greater leadership responsibilities in the future (Berman, 2008; Reeves, 2009b). For the current purposes, however, I will accept that hierarchy in educational organizations is a fact of life, and therefore readers are better served not with the illusion of an absent hierarchy but with a realistic vision of how hierarchies can be less toxic (Hamel, 2009) and more effective.

The pyramid is an excellent example of the impact of hierarchy because of its structural and mathematical properties. Whereas a triangle illustrates to some degree the top-down structure of hierarchy, it fails to show the magnitude of the impact that decisions at the top have on other levels of the organization. Imagine that you are at the bottom of a triangle, with a single line—the base of the triangle—pressing against you. It's uncomfortable, but, depending on where that line hits your body, it is bearable. Contrast that feeling with being at the bottom of a solid pyramid. The weight of the structure covers your entire body. You can't move and you can't breathe. Struggle against the weight of the pyramid is futile. You don't need a mathematical equation to sense that the weight of the pyramid can be suffocating. The impact of one person or a small group at the top of the organization on everyone else can be

**FIGURE 6.5**  The Pyramidal Organization

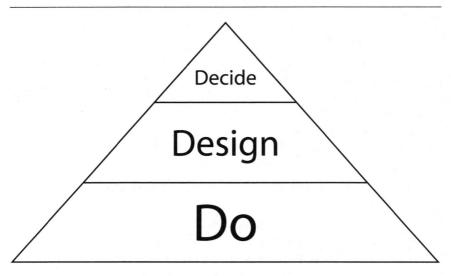

overwhelming. It is not only the weight of the pyramid that matters, but also the complexity. The greater the number of potential power combinations in the pyramid at the higher levels, the less likely it is that the people at the lower levels will understand and communicate with those in power. To have some fun illustrating the impact of decisions by leaders in your organization, do the math at http://mathworld.wolfram.com/ SquarePyramid.html. In fact, even a typical pyramid, such as that illustrated in Figure 6.5, understates the complexity of the challenge because the size of the base of the pyramid in schools can be enormously larger than the top level of school systems, states, and the federal government, with dozens, even hundreds of schools influenced by the hierarchy.

Servant leadership represents an inversion of the pyramid. Servant leaders understand their role not as "command and control" but as servants of a worthy mission and vision. Although much as been written about the notion of servant leadership (Greenleaf, Spears, & Covey, 2002), the concept is more widely described than practiced. The rather crude progress from Decide (top leadership), to Design (mid-level administrators), to Do (workers) is redolent of factories from the Industrial Revolution of the 19th century and, indeed, some schools of the 21st century look and sound very much like those factories. But just as hierarchy need not be toxic, it also need not be pyramidal in nature. The

**FIGURE 6.6** From the Pyramid to the Diamond

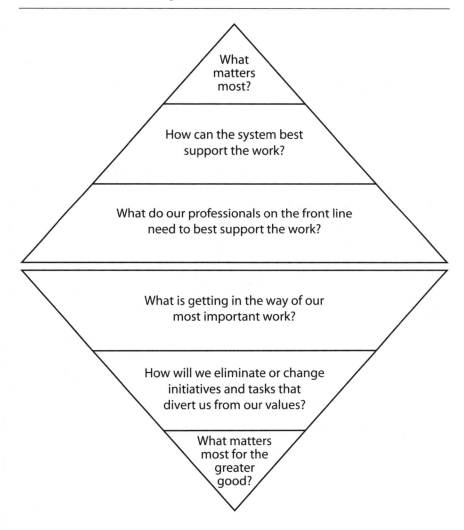

lessons of leadership focus offer a different perspective. It is the job of leadership to contribute to a compelling vision and focused mission, but this need not be the exclusive purview of senior administrators and policymakers. Moreover, because of the proliferating impact of leadership decisions on the bottom of the pyramid, it is clearly the responsibility of senior leaders to help create focus throughout the organization, changing the metaphor from a pyramid to a diamond (see Figure 6.6).

Not only is this different, but the Decide, Design, Do model is replaced by a process infused with inquiry, challenge, and focus.

In the Decide, Design, Do model, the clear message to teachers is that their job is execution of decisions that have already been made. This model excludes inquiry and reflection and, as a result, makes continuous improvement nearly impossible. To the extent that evaluation of decisions and processes takes place, it is an evaluation either by organizations near the top of the pyramid or by external organizations. While there is clearly an important role for evaluation by both senior leaders and external evaluators, the essence of the diamond is that evaluation and inquiry are continuous processes at every level, from the boardroom to the classroom.

Inviting inquiry does not mean anarchy. Leadership retains the responsibility for synthesizing the needs of many stakeholders and then focusing the entire organization on the best means to achieve its goals.

In this chapter I have laid the groundwork for gaining leadership focus at the system level. In the next chapter, I will address how to apply the principles of leadership focus for schools, with a particular focus on the needs of principals and teacher-leaders.

---
CHAPTER 7
---

# Focus at the School Level

**E**FFECTIVE LEADERSHIP at the school level is not merely about articulating a vision, though vision is surely important. It is not just about articulating and executing strategy, though those skills are also important. Strategy, as Michael Porter (1980) and Kim and Mauborgne (2005) remind us, is not merely about deciding what to do but also about deciding what not to do. For school leaders enduring the withering assault of initiative proliferation, the challenge of focus may seem insurmountable. After all, they are near the bottom of the hierarchical pyramid of a traditional school system and, along with classroom teachers, they bear the brunt of multiple demands of policy, procedure, and prescription. Yet it is possible for a school to engage in effective focus, as the following discussion will demonstrate. By asking the right questions, focusing on the factors with the greatest leverage, guarding a culture of success, and embracing the power of teacher leadership, school leaders can be at the point of a diamond rather than at the bottom of a pyramid.

## Essential Questions Revisited

In the previous chapter I identified two essential questions:

- What is the extent of my ability to influence this action?
- What impact will this action have on the student learning results I am seeking to achieve?

These questions come into sharper focus for leaders at the school level. To address the first question, leaders must pose a more basic question to every staff member: "What causes student achievement?" Take a moment and list all of the causes of student achievement that you can think of in Figure 7.1. Ideally, this is a task done in a professional learning community, or other gathering of teachers and administrators, brainstorming as many different causes as you can think of.

When you consider the items on the list, you will notice a wide range of elements of student achievement, ranging from leadership strategies

**FIGURE 7.1**   Brainstorming the Causes of Student Achievement

| | | |
|---|---|---|
| *Instructions:* List as many causes of student achievement as you can think of below. This is a brainstorming activity, so do not filter out the causes, but consider your personal experience and professional reading to identify as many causes as you can think of. | | |
| | | |
| | | |
| | | |
| | | |
| | | |
| | | |
| | | |
| | | |
| | | |
| | | |

to teacher expectations to home environments. But when you reconsider your list in light of the first essential question, and ask "What are the *primary* causes of student achievement?" a pattern will quickly emerge. All of the causes you identified are either subject to your influence or they are not. Some factors—such as the frequency of feedback to students, the creation of multiple opportunities for success, and the monitoring and delivery of effective teaching practices—are clearly within the leader's sphere of influence. Other factors—such as the extent to which students were exposed to reading as infants or were subjected to lead paint, alcohol, or drugs before birth—are clearly outside the leader's influence. But many other factors are on a continuum and, upon further consideration, will be found to be more subject to leadership influence than they might at first have appeared.

Consider the example of student attendance. While our visceral reaction to the causes of student attendance or absence may be that it is a matter determined wholly by students and their families, there is abundant research that suggests that leadership policies and practices have a significant impact on attendance (Erickson, 2010; Reeves, 2008b). The same is true of parental involvement. While some claim that this is a factor controlled exclusively by families, we also know that the same parents are more communicative with some leaders and teachers than with others. This means there must be something about the leadership and teaching practices, not just the behavior of the parents, that encourages or diminishes parental involvement. For example, schools in Broad Award–winning Norfolk, Virginia, have created Father's Clubs to engage fathers who often have not been engaged in their children's schools. Teachers and administrators in Milwaukee make home visits to families who have been unable to attend parent–teacher conferences. Schools in areas where parents are undocumented workers have held meetings in church basements or other facilities that are regarded by parents as "safe" in order to promote better connections between parents and schools. John Goodlad's (1984, 1990) seminal research on more than 2,500 schools makes clear that even when parents, students, faculties, and budgets are consistent, leadership is a singularly important variable at the school level, and the most effective leaders have widespread influence on factors far beyond administrative decisions. Revisit your list of the causes of student achievement and organize them into two columns, representing those factors a leader can influence and those

factors that are beyond the influence of the leader. Enter these results
in Figure 7.2.

This analysis is very revealing, and it bears directly on the application
of expectation theory—the well-established psychological principle that
"we get what we expect" from children, for better or worse. High expectations beget higher performance; low expectations lead to lower performance. If your entries in Figure 7.2 are disproportionately on the

**FIGURE 7.2**   Causes of Student Achievement Reconsidered

| Causes Influenced by Leaders | Causes Beyond the Leader's Influence |
|---|---|
|  |  |
|  |  |
|  |  |
|  |  |
|  |  |
|  |  |
|  |  |
|  |  |
|  |  |
|  |  |
|  |  |
|  |  |
|  |  |

left-hand side, representing factors within the leader's sphere of influence, then you are demonstrating a high degree of efficacy, the conviction that your personal work influences the results. Disproportionate numbers of entries on the right-hand side suggest the opposite. What is particularly interesting is that you can create a professional learning activity with staff members using Figures 7.1 and 7.2 when considering the same group of students and nevertheless get strikingly different results—even as the poverty rate, second language rate, and environmental factors are identical. Then the evidence is clear that the variable is not the students or the causes associated with their achievement, but the leader's and staff members' perceptions of influence.

The second essential question regards the impact of leadership actions on student achievement and other key goals. Here is where leaders have the opportunity to identify the key leverage points for focus. Schools around the world claim to be "doing Marzano" by virtue of embracing the thoughtful and excellent teaching strategies resulting from the meta-analysis accomplished by Marzano and his colleagues (Marzano, 2007; Marzano, Pickering, & Pollock, 2001; Marzano et al., 2005). But even excellent research can yield terrible practice, particularly when leaders fail to focus on the actions with the highest degree of leverage. For example, Marzano's research strongly suggests that feedback to students is a critically important instructional variable, provided that the feedback is accurate, timely, and specific. In fact, successful feedback is synergistic, providing support and reinforcement for other teaching strategies. Conversely, even the best curriculum and assessment systems will be of little value if students do not receive feedback that is accurate, timely, and specific. Schools are littered with very sophisticated assessments that approach psychometric perfection and, viewed in isolation, appear to be excellent tools. But if the feedback from those assessments is not provided to students in a timely manner, then it is impossible for students and teachers to use that excellent information. If the feedback is generic—principals report average scores for the building but are afraid to report the results of individual students and teachers—then the impact is no greater than if we attempted to reduce teenage obesity by reporting only the average weight, average diet, and average exercise behaviors for students for the entire school. Strangely, however, it is rare for a school leader to focus on this singularly important variable—feedback that focuses on individuals as well as whole school numbers.

Another example of ineffectual translation of research into practice is the use of checklists for the application of instructional practices without a consideration of the context of those practices. In "Setting the Record Straight on 'High-Yield' Strategies," Marzano (2009b) tersely noted:

> Checklist approaches to providing feedback to teachers probably don't enhance pedagogical expertise, particularly when they focus on a narrow list of instructional management, or assessment strategies. In fact, such practice is antithetical to true reflective practice. (p. 37)

How can leaders assess their degree of effective focus? First, leaders can measure the results they wish to achieve in consistent and clear manners. Second, leaders can describe the performance that they expect on a continuum, from exemplary to unacceptable. For example, leaders can report data on feedback in the following ways:

- The number of times a teacher provided specific feedback to students during a classroom observation.
- The number of times students used the feedback to make immediate improvements in their performance.
- The number of times students used the feedback systems of the classroom, such as a scoring rubric, to provide feedback to one another that led to immediate improvements in performance.
- The number of times students used feedback systems to provide self-assessment that led to immediate improvements in performance.

Beyond measurement, leaders can also describe a continuum of performance. Imagine a group of six music teachers. The first has students play through the Minuet in G with the blissful ignorance of Professor Harold Hill in *The Music Man*, oblivious to the off-key, groaning sounds emanating from their instruments. Devoid of feedback, the ensemble plods onward, offending the ears of all but the most tone-deaf and adoring parents. The second teacher endures the same performance, but at the end of the period, provides an eviscerating critique. There is feedback, but the results are not much better. The third teacher provides a lacerating critique after each measure of music, and then moves on to the next phrase. While the last two teachers in this example might claim to be providing feedback to students, they hardly meet the standards that Marzano or any good instructional leader has in mind.

A fourth teacher provides feedback, but also provides the group an opportunity to immediately apply the feedback once, twice, three times or more, practicing and hearing the improvements each time. Colvin (2008) observes that it is this practice method more than innate talent that separates the best musicians from those who are mediocre. A fifth teacher also provides feedback immediately followed by opportunities for success, but in addition provides small group routines that allow students to listen to one another, provide feedback, and improve individual and small group performance. A sixth teacher not only incorporates these feedback and repetition strategies but also equips students to apply the same techniques when practicing alone.

The same degree of variation in the quality and quantity of feedback can be observed in any subject. Some teachers of writing provide excellent critiques, but they are delivered 3 weeks after the students wrote their essays and the grading system provides no incentive for students to use the critiques to revise their work multiple times and improve their performance. Some athletic coaches yell critiques while others identify a particular movement, isolate it, and practice it until it is so ingrained in students' understanding that they can not only respond to instructions from the coach, but they can also give equally clear coaching to one another and to themselves. Because the impact of feedback is so universal, it is a clear candidate for leadership focus. When feedback is done well, it has a dramatic, clear, and measurable impact on student performance. When feedback is not done well, it undermines everything else the teacher is attempting to do.

## Individual Students

One of the less helpful false dichotomies to infect the leadership literature is the distinction between "strategic" and "tactical" leadership, the former summoning images of Patton, Clausewitz, and Lao Tzu, and the latter a shop foreman issuing orders on the assembly line. Who wouldn't rather focus on grand strategy? But the research on leadership focus tells a different story. The wise teacher is able both to analyze the impact of a lesson or engagement strategy on the class as a whole and also to identify the learning needs of individual students. Similarly, focused leaders are able to consider student data from two perspectives—which we can call the vertical and the horizontal perspectives. Imagine a large wall chart that lists students' names in the left-hand column, and shows students' objectives for learning and behavior across the top. Some of the columns might refer to persuasive writing, while others might apply to organization, number operations, teamwork, scientific inquiry, and so on. The "vertical" question for each column focuses on the general objective: finding out how our students as a whole are doing in reading comprehension, fluency, and project management. When there are general trends that show success, leaders have a clue toward effective practice that can be identified, documented, and replicated. When there are general trends that suggest trouble, then the focus is not on the characteristics of the student. The vertically focused leader does not hear the excuse, "The kids just aren't working on it," when the vertical analysis of the column shows widespread failure among a large number of students.

The horizontal focus, by contrast, is on the individual student. In this example, each row represents an individual student, and the horizontal perspective gives clues for improved student success. For example, do we notice that many instances of low performance in math and science are accompanied by struggles in reading comprehension? If so, before we engage in a frantic series of fragmentary interventions, perhaps it is necessary to give the student concentrated support in improved reading skills. If we notice that low performance is also associated with poor time and project management strategies, then the student needs help with study skills, not just with subject matter knowledge. How is it possible for school leaders to maintain a horizontal focus, particularly as schools consolidate and the ratio of students to administrators rises? In fact, one of the consistent hallmarks of effective school leaders is the combination of vertical and horizontal focuses, and that includes a consideration of individual students (Smith, 2008). The leaders know the names of students, talk with parents, and perhaps even teach a class. These leaders personally review report cards, learning plans, and portfolios of students. Their daily disciplines include one-to-one meetings with students not just for disciplinary infractions but to talk about goals, dreams, and concerns. Even the busiest school leader has time for two 15-minute meetings per day with individual students, a schedule that yields 360 meetings each year. Even in a school of 1,000 students, this student-focused leader will have had the opportunity for a scheduled one-to-one meeting with every student during a 3-year span of time. Of course, student focus requires more than an annual meeting, and thus leaders committed to focus help create small groups of students who build relationships with adults and one another. Even in large and complex secondary schools with thousands of students, leaders can engage every staff member, including noncertified staff, to develop multi-year relationships with students so that there are always adults in the school who know every student by name, call them when they miss school, and offer an attentive ear. If you think the scale of your school is too large for this level of student focus by administrators, try this exercise:

N = Total student population
S = Total staff members, including faculty, administrators, paraprofessionals, and support staff

What is N divided by S?

Even in large and seemingly ungovernable schools where leaders have traditionally been removed from the lives of all but the most outstanding and most troubled students, the N/S calculation reveals a golden opportunity for engagement and relationships. Because the N/S ratio typically ranges from 12 to 15, we have the opportunity to ask each staff member to simply know and care about a relatively small group of students. These staff members have the students' pictures, call out to them in the hallway, share a quick glass of milk during lunch, and ask about their siblings, pets, parents, and interests. It is no accident that such purposeful relationship building is a key when complex urban systems show dramatically reduced failures (Reeves, 2006b). No one is asking the school secretary, cafeteria manager, network administrator, or custodian to be a counselor or classroom teacher, but it is entirely reasonable to ask each of these support professionals to know and care about a small group of students, to greet them warmly, and to notice them.

## Teaching Quality

Although "instructional leadership" is a popular phrase, it is maddeningly difficult and rare for leaders to define teacher quality with consistency and precision. The terms "walk-through," "learning walk," and a cluster of similar phrases generally refer to attempts of administrators and teacher-leaders to quickly observe classroom instruction, the learning activities of students, and the cultural environment of a school and class-room. These are laudable goals if they are done well, and prescriptions for disaster if they are done badly. The promise of an effective observa-tion is that when there are clear mutual understandings of the elements of effective teaching, then administrators, teachers, and teacher-leaders can collaborate to document and celebrate effective practice and objec-tively address deficiencies in practice. With such a common understand-ing, a focus on the essentials of effective practice should be the natural result. Unfortunately, the reality for the vast majority of schools I have observed is strikingly different. Consider the following real examples from educational systems that prefer to remain anonymous:

- After a $1.2 million investment in training in observation, a large urban district abandoned the program in less than 2 years. In many schools, the observations for which administrators were trained never started.
- In another urban system, "swat teams" of observers were deployed to observe one classroom in every building and rate teachers on each of four critical elements of instruction. The teams made their observations, returned to the central office, and then, 2 months later, posted the results in a high school gymnasium. There was no discussion, no personal feedback, no analysis—just the posting of the results.
- Technology must be the answer, reasoned one district, so in order to make the observations easier, they purchased hand-held digital devices to allow administrators to quickly make observations and systematically record and report the data. The computers were purchased, the training was delivered, and the boxes of very expensive materials arrived in each school. Months later, I found four boxes of these materials in one school—unopened, sitting in a corner of the principal's private bathroom.

In each of these and many other cases, what began as an attempt to focus on "teacher quality" morphed into one more evanescent program that consumed resources and time, and then vanished. There must be a better way. The best example of leadership focus on teacher quality is represented by the "mini-observation" instrument developed by Kim Marshall (2010) and shared for use in schools around the world. The rubrics are designed to be an end-of-year summative evaluation tool after the principal has made a number of unannounced mini-observations (ideally 10–12) over the course of the year and has had formative conversations with each teacher. The observer can simply highlight the lines on the observation form that correspond to teacher practice. If the observer does not see a practice, that line is left blank. The mini-observations are made throughout the year so that they can be used as formative feedback designed not only to evaluate a teacher but also to improve practice, and they are a way to capture reality and give teachers frequent, helpful feedback. The rubrics are a good way to sum up performance on a 4-3-2-1 scale, with specific descriptions at the end of the year. More detailed information can be found at www.MarshallMemo.com. For those who wish to lead by example, Marshall has also created a set of mini-observation rubrics for principals. These are available as Resource E in *Assessing Educational Leaders*, 2nd edition (Reeves, 2009a).

## Conclusion

The case for leadership focus is compelling at every level. In this chapter, I have offered the evidence that finding your leadership focus is an imperative not only to improve student achievement but also to improve staff morale. It is tempting to blame leadership diffusion on higher levels of authority and take the side of the beleaguered and overwhelmed principal and teacher. In fact, leaders at every level, including teacher-leaders in the classroom, own a central role in replacing diffusion with focus. This requires choices in time, teaching strategies, traditions, and relationships.

In sum, I would argue that focus is the first obligation of leaders. With it, we can meet our most important goals and find the energy to care for students and colleagues. Without it, no amount of wishful thinking, imperious demands, threats of accountability, external mandates, or good intentions will be sufficient.

## CHAPTER 8

# How Leaders Can Help Classroom Teachers to Focus, Save Time, and Improve Achievement

"**W**E DON'T HAVE THE TIME.**" These words crystallize the most frequent complaint of classroom teachers, a reflection not only of my personal conversations with teachers around the world but also of a recent large-scale analysis by Ingersoll and Perda (2009), a study that challenges the frequent assertion that financial considerations alone are at the heart of teacher dissatisfaction. Inadequate preparation time and insufficient influence on decision-making were found to be consistent and pervasive sources of dissatisfaction among teachers who leave the profession. The researchers considered the particular cases of teachers in math and science, where shortages of certified teachers are most acute. Was the root cause of the shortage inadequate compensation? Poor discipline? Attractive alternatives in the private sector? In fact, of 13 sources of dissatisfaction considered by the analysis, inadequate time to prepare was the leading cause of dissatisfaction for teachers outside of math and science (60%), the leading cause of dissatisfaction for science teachers (69.3%), and the leading cause of dissatisfaction for math teachers (67.5%). This factor outdistances salary benefits, student behavioral problems, large class sizes, and difficulties due to mainstreaming special students, to name just a few. Complementary to the Ingersoll and Perda study are the findings of Pink (2009) that the ability to influence decisions, along with professional autonomy, is key to teacher satisfaction. In other words, educational leaders and policymakers can make a large number of changes to improve the lives of teaching professionals, but if they fail to address the fundamental issue of focus—giving classroom teachers more time to focus on fewer priorities and giving teachers a voice in what those priorities are—then that failure to focus will undermine every other reform.

This chapter offers five practical methods teachers can use to improve classroom focus and save time. These strategies are power standards, collaborative scoring, parallel rubrics, assignment menus, and early examinations.

## Too Many Standards, Too Little Time

Marzano and Kendall (1998) analyzed early versions of state standards and found that there were too many standards for the time available in school systems around the nation. Since that analysis, a few states have suggested that some standards might have priority over others, but the clear trend has been for greater detail and longer lists of requirements, all crammed into a school year that remains based on the notion that after 180 days of class and the summer solstice, students must return to their families' farms and help till the soil. The Common Core Standards, published for comment in early 2010 by the National Governors Association and The Council of Chief State School Officers, are more focused than those imposed by most individual states. However, the devil remains in the details, and states retain the prerogative to use the Common Core Standards as only one part of their required curriculum. With each addition made within the confines of a fixed school schedule, there are fewer minutes available for teachers and students to concentrate on individual learning objectives.

The result of burgeoning state standards and bloated textbooks has been, at the classroom level, curriculum by default. Decisions about what content to include and what to omit are a combination of personal preferences, traditions, and the exhaustion of available days on the calendar. Even changes to school calendars that appear to be "time neutral," such as a change to block scheduling, can have a devastating impact on curriculum when, for example, a class is changed from 180 periods of 47 minutes a day to 90 periods of 94 minutes every other day. While the number of instructional minutes in both schedules should be equal, the new schedule ultimately leads to a series of 60-minute classes and 30-minute study periods. Not surprisingly, the end of the year arrives and significant parts of the curriculum have yet to be considered.

This is not merely a matter of time management. Academic content standards are created by political bodies and, inevitably, reflect political priorities. Whether standards are set at the local, state, or national level, the requirement that a body of knowledge is taught in school reflects a political and cultural priority. The omission of any specific learning objective, however, does not imply that it is disrespected by political powers and irrelevant to the culture. Logic, as is often the case in educational debates, has little to do with it. The partisans of specific learning objectives, from the Declaration of Independence to the properties of the rhombus, will argue for the inclusion of their favorite content, the time available notwithstanding. Therefore, teachers need practical ways to save time and improve focus.

## Power Standards

To determine which academic standards deserve the greatest investment of classroom time, teachers should ask three questions. First, which standards have leverage—that is, which knowledge and skill requirements have applicability to multiple disciplines? Second, which standards have endurance—that is, which knowledge and skills will be useful not merely to answer a specific test question, but to form the basis for building future knowledge? Third, which standards are most essential for the next level of learning?

### Standards with Leverage

Some skills, such as reading and writing, are obvious. Because students must engage in descriptive and analytical writing in science, social studies, English, math, and many other disciplines, it makes sense that these literacy skills should consume a disproportionate amount of curriculum time. But this rarely happens. A national study (Kiuhara, Graham, & Hawken, 2009) recently confirmed more than a decade of research showing that nonfiction writing skills were imperative for success not only in secondary school but also in the workplace, in technical schools, and in universities. Unfortunately, the researchers also found that most evidence-based writing strategies are too rarely employed in classrooms devoted to English language arts and are almost never used in science, mathematics, and social studies classes. Similarly, critical reasoning—the heart of hypothesis testing in science and the expression of proofs in mathematics—is a skill that has leverage in every academic area. The pictorial representation of information using graphs, charts, tables, and other images is essential in mathematics but also has broad applicability in the social sciences. The essential case for power standards is that some standards are more important than others. No matter how many or how few curriculum expectations teachers face, they know that it is more important for students to master descriptive writing than to read science fiction; it is more important to express and test hypotheses than to explode a plastic volcano; and it is more important to master the creation and interpretation of charts and graphs than it is to distinguish the rhombus from the parallelogram. These are the practical choices that teachers must make every day. Instead of platitudes about working smarter, they need a systematic means for identifying what is most important for students to learn.

## Standards for Learning with Enduring Value

The concept of enduring value refers to the importance of knowledge and skills over time. Games like Jeopardy! and Trivial Pursuit emphasize the value of short-term knowledge, whereas power standards elevate the importance of knowledge and skills with endurance. In the game of Jeopardy! it is essential to know that the Battle of Hastings took place in 1066; in real life, it is essential to understand that Thomas Jefferson was not the first person to object to tyrants. In the first game, it is essential to know the year in which the War of 1812 began and the length of the 100 Years War; in the second "game" it is essential know that colonial power is persistent and that young democracies do not necessarily emerge from colonial rule with a single document and or a decisive war. Evanescent standards require that a student memorize the trigonometric formulae for three types of right triangles but never think about the practical difference between a 30-60-90 triangle and a 45-45-90 triangle again a nanosecond after the completion of a standardized test. Enduring standards require that students understand a single formula—such as the Pythagorean theorem—and discern applications for it in geography, navigation, economics, educational leadership, and psychology.

Students will use the Pythagorean theorem when they need to know the distance between two points, whether it is to plan a hike in the woods or a cross-country solo flight. As economists, they will use the same theorem to calculate the distance between points on a graph of consumer behavior and a line that predicts that behavior. As educational leaders or psychologists, they will evaluate research and statistics claims, many of which trace their mathematical origin to the work of Pythagorus. Whether they are looking at a map or a graph, they are evaluating the distance between two points.

### Standards Necessary for the Next Level of Learning

Ask a fourth-grade teacher "What curriculum content are you willing to give up?" The almost certain response is "Nothing—everything I do is important. Besides, whatever I eliminate might be on the test at the end of the year. And if I fail to cover everything in the curriculum, I risk being punished by administrators." Ask the same teacher, however, to give advice to a third-grade teacher about the knowledge and skills that third-grade students must acquire in order to enter fourth grade with confidence and success. The response is never "Everything is important, and you must cover it all because it might be on the test at the end of the year." On the contrary, the advice given by fourth-grade teachers to their counterparts in the third grade is focused and brief. The advice from fourth-grade teachers will consider not only the imperatives of literacy and math, but also the need for organizing a project, keeping an assignment notebook, asking good questions, and seeking help when necessary. The gap between what is necessary and what is taught is most evident in the transitional years between middle school and high school. While many middle school curricula emphasize coverage of standards in the middle grades, high school teachers might suggest that teamwork, integrity, personal responsibility, and critical thinking are more essential than the assurance that students have covered every eighth-grade standard. While middle school teachers routinely struggle with a fragmented schedule and curriculum, their colleagues in the first years of high school express consistent concerns that incoming students need basic skills in reading, writing, math, time management, and personal organization.

### Power Standards in Practice

In order to determine whether power standards have potential for saving teachers time, two tests can be applied. The first is a comparison of the content of power standards to end-of-year test content. In a growing number of jurisdictions, prior summative assessments are matters of public record and therefore teachers do not need to speculate about what might be on the test—it is on the state's Department of Education website and available to any interested party. The second test of the time-saving value of power standards is a commonsense appeal to teachers in higher grades to examine the curriculum and assessment system in the lower grades. One example of the application of this test occurred in a school system I visited in the southwestern United States. There were more than 90 discrete math requirements for eighth-grade students. Teachers collaborated to create the following power standards:

1. Number operations—add, subtract, multiply, and divide—with and without a calculator.
2. Tables, charts, and graphs—given a data set, create them; given the visual representation, draw accurate inferences from them.
3. Given a story problem, draw a picture that accurately reflects the problem.
4. Properties (area and perimeter) of rectangles and triangles.
5. Linear, area, and volume measurements in metric and English systems.

When this list was presented to curriculum designers for the eighth grade, the response was abrupt and negative. "You left out the rhombus!" they protested. "What about probability?" complained another. To be sure, questions on the rhombus and probability were among the items that had appeared on previous state tests. Indeed, an analysis of those tests revealed that 12% of the items on the tests were not addressed by this list of power standards. I know of few eighth-grade teachers who would not happily settle for a greater opportunity to help students achieve proficiency on the remainder of the curriculum. This level of focus does not guarantee success, but it does allocate the time of teachers and students in a more rational manner. They have the opportunity to achieve an 88% percent level of mastery on a math test, particularly when compared to the alternative—minimal proficiency by students associated with claims of comprehensive coverage by exhausted teachers. When the same list was presented to ninth-grade math teachers, the response was unanimous: "If only our incoming algebra students could know these five power standards, then they would be successful in our classes."

In sum, power standards represent the essence of focus at the class-room level. Educational leaders cannot talk a good game about focus, and then foist 500-page textbooks, frantic pacing guides, and overloaded standards documents onto classroom teachers. Administrators and teachers must collaborate to address the three essential questions of power standards: What has leverage? What endures? What is most important for the next level of learning?

## Collaborative Scoring

What could possibly go wrong with such a feel-good concept as collaboration? Teachers are social beings, they enjoy working together, and collaboration is a widely valued social norm. It should be easy—but it isn't. Collaboration, like most challenging skills, requires practice and persistence. Nevertheless, when done well, it not only improves classroom results but saves teachers time. The evidence for this claim comes from a series of four experiments I conducted with the same group of California classroom teachers. They were given the same samples of student work from 12 different students and asked to use a common rubric to score the work. The results from the initial meeting were miserable—the level of agreement among the teachers was 19%, based on the number of teachers who reached the same conclusion (a score of 1, 2, 3, or 4) on the 12 samples of work. Worse yet, the teachers worked at a glacial pace, completing the scoring in approximately 45 minutes. Because these were fairly simple one-page assignments, the combination of low levels of agreement and a heavy time commitment required of individual teachers for scoring was not sustainable.

In the conversations among teachers during the course of collaborative scoring, and that followed, things went from bad to worse. Collaboration, it turns out, is neither natural nor easy. There were strongly held opinions—many of them well reasoned but not included in the scoring rubric—on why each teacher reached different conclusions about the scores on the student work. After some discussion, we reached an important insight: The enemy is not one another; the enemy is ambiguity. Whereas many collaborative conversations become combative, with one professional attempting to change the mind of another, these conversations changed in focus. Rather than a comparison of opinions and contentious statements about whose standards were better, the teachers focused their conversation on a direct comparison of the student work under consideration and the specifications of the scoring rubric. "We're intelligent and capable people. How could we look at the same piece of student work and come to such different conclusions? The answer must be in the ambiguity of the scoring rubric."

As the participants in these experiments worked to move from ambiguity to clarity, four remarkable outcomes occurred. First, the quality and specificity of the scoring rubrics improved. Second, the degree of agreement among classroom teachers increased from 19% to 92% by the conclusion of the fourth meeting. Third, and most importantly, the quality of the student work—the same students were engaged in the entire experiment, except for minimal mobility—improved dramatically, perhaps because they were receiving feedback that was more clear and specific. Fourth—and the finding most relevant to teachers' complaints— the time required for the teachers to score the same quantity of student work declined from 45 minutes to 9 minutes. The length of the student assignments was the same—in fact, the length of the student work increased somewhat. But the ability of teachers to quickly assess the work had grown remarkably. Rather than taking 45 minutes to reach a low level of consensus, teachers looking at a similar quantity of student work reached a high level of consensus within 9 minutes.

Consider for a moment all of the professional development experiences for teachers that you have observed. Which ones saved time and increased effectiveness? Which ones added to the burdens and time commitments of teachers? Which ones added to the responsibilities of teachers, but failed to add necessary support, including time in the schedule, to meet those responsibilities? Even well-intended professional development experiences can be formulas for frustration if we accept the proposition that "training equals learning."

Consider this alternative proposition: "Professional learning will be difficult and intellectually challenging. But if we persist and engage in this work, we will not only increase the quality of student work and the degree of consistency with our colleagues, but we will also use our time more efficiently and reduce the total time burdens that are currently placed on teachers and administrators." This proposition represents an exceptional challenge, but it is achievable if our analysis of professional practices includes not only "training" but also the complete context of professional learning, including:

1. Time required for all current professional development programs and requirements.
2. Time required for learning, practicing, and assessing new professional learning. In this context, we are considering not only the assessment of students, but the assessment of how teachers and administrators implement the new professional learning.
3. Opportunities for midcourse corrections in the new professional learning, based upon the feedback we receive in the course of practice and assessment.
4. Conscious decisions to remove burdens of time, practice, and tradition in order to ensure that we have sufficient time for learning, assessment, feedback, and midcourse corrections.

## *Parallel Rubrics*

After watching a first-grade teacher in Alaska (*Video Journal of Education*, 1999) allow students to create their own scoring rubrics, I was inspired to use three-column rubrics for students at levels ranging from second grade to doctoral level. While the complexity is obviously different at each level, my work with elementary and doctoral students shares this common characteristic: Students learn more when they first assess their own work, guided by a clear and explicit scoring rubric. This is in stark contrast to the traditional practice in which the student is the worker and the teacher is the inspector. While clearly I expect to challenge students and give them helpful feedback, they are best served when they learn to carefully and explicitly assess their own work. This practice dramatically shortens the interval between submission of student work and the teacher's response. A three-column parallel rubric for student assessment is shown in Figure 8.1. The left-hand column represents the requirements of the work in student-accessible language. For example, the first-grade classroom required that "every sentence must end with appropriate punctuation." A doctoral-level rubric might well include, based on my experience, the same admonition that the first-graders received, but could also include "Conclusions are based upon a combination of multiple methodologies" or "Conclusions consider both the strengths and weaknesses of alternative methodological approaches." The middle column represents the student's self-assessment for each requirement. When the first-grade student notices the omission of a comma, period, or question mark, he or she might return to the desk

**FIGURE 8.1**   Example of a Parallel Rubric

| Learning Objective: Use evidence to support an argument | | |
|---|---|---|
| Note to Teachers: Practice by having students assess the work of other students they do not know. Students must know how to use the rubric in an accurate and consistent manner in order to make this an effective learning and assessment tool for themselves. | | |
| **Performance Levels** | **Student Self-Assessment** | **Teacher Review\*** |
| **Not meeting standards** | | |
| The speaker or writer did not use evidence to support the argument. | | |
| **Progressing** | | |
| There is limited evidence— such as one or two statistics— to support the argument. | | |
| The link between the evidence and the argument is not clear. | | |
| The argument is not important and does not grab the attention of the listener or reader. | | |
| **Proficient** | | |
| The argument is a clear statement supported with factual evidence. | | |
| The evidence includes both statistics and examples. | | |
| The evidence is linked to the argument in a clear and logical way. | | |
| The writer or speaker provides persuasive reasons that the argument is important—that is, the issue is important for society to consider. | | |

*(continued on the next page)*

**FIGURE 8.1**   Example of a Parallel Rubric (*continued*)

| Performance Levels | Student Self-Assessment | Teacher Review* |
|---|---|---|
| **Exemplary** | | |
| The writer or speaker begins with a compelling introduction, making clear why the argument is important. | | |
| There is a clear argument expressed in the form of a statement that can be supported with, or attacked with, evidence. | | |
| The evidence includes relevant statistics, examples, and conclusions by qualified experts. | | |
| The writer or speaker clearly links each piece of evidence to the argument in a compelling and persuasive way. | | |
| The writer or speaker concludes with a compelling reason for the reader or listener to agree, applying the evidence and argument to a particular example. | | |
| **Additional comments** | | |
| | | |
| *Check mark used to indicate that the teacher agrees with the student self-assessment. | | |

and repair the error before submitting the work to the teacher. When the doctoral fellow notices that the wild enthusiasm expressed for a case study was not accompanied by a conflicting conclusion from a meta-analysis or quantitative study, he or she might return to the library and add a few clarifying paragraphs. The right-hand column is the only one filled in by the teacher, and the only marks necessary are where the evaluations of the student and teacher diverge. Because the expectations have already been expressed clearly and consistently in the left-hand column, the teacher is no longer writing the same comment on dozens of papers. Thus the feedback is clear, consistent, and fast. Most importantly, it not only saves the teacher's time, but it also helps students become more reflective assessors of their own work.

How does this work in practice? When I must focus on an original analysis of an entire paper, I am tempted to write an essay, hoping that my students will take my words to heart and use this personalized feedback to improve their performance. It is a time-consuming process, and a potentially long interval will elapse between the student's submission of the work and receipt of my feedback. When, by contrast, I use the parallel rubric system, I focus only on the areas where the student and I disagree. The practical impact is that the time from submission of work to feedback can be reduced from 7 days (an eternity in the lives of college students and a second in the lives of their professors) to 1 day. For public school students, this technique can be used to provide same-day feedback—not quite the speed of the video games to which our students are accustomed, but nevertheless much faster than the typical response time from teachers.

## Assignment Menus

Researchers strongly disagree about the value of homework (Kohn, 2006; Marzano & Pickering, 2007). Despite these divergent views, however, two conclusions seem inescapable. First, in order for students to master challenging skills, they must practice them. Second, a great deal of homework fails to achieve this objective either because it is dull and repetitious, requiring practice of skills the students have already mastered, or because it is incomprehensible, leading students to abandon the task in frustration or practice doing it wrong. Students differ not only in their cognitive readiness for many homework assignments but also in their organizational readiness. The latter is often related not merely to the organizational discipline of the students but to the attentiveness of their parents. The result is that teachers waste a great deal of time assigning and evaluating student work that does not lead to improved learning. One strategy to address these challenges is the use of an assignment menu.

The assignment menu provides two types of choices for students—choices of topics and choices of size of individual assignments. These choices take place within appropriate boundaries, of course. Whatever the choice made by the students, they must master the academic content that the teacher expects and they must do approximately the same amount of work in order to earn the same amount of credit.

Consider this hypothetical Grade 9 American Studies (a joint history and English class) assignment. Students are required to complete a major research paper, including a consideration of at least five secondary sources, three historical documents, and three U.S. Supreme Court cases that are relevant to the question. The first choice that students have is of topic. Students must choose a controversy of historical significance that has been considered by the Supreme Court. Their paper must address the source of the conflict, its historical context, the manner in which it was resolved, and the student's analysis of the strengths and weaknesses of the Court's conclusion. If student choice stopped here, then teachers would receive the typical stack of papers, almost all on the same day, and because these major assignments are typically done at the end of the year, the teachers would labor for hours to evaluate them, with some even providing feedback to the students. But the teachers' hours of work are often futile, because students are unable to use the feedback to improve their performance. Some students will submit exemplary work, perhaps aided by college-educated parents who reviewed and revised several drafts before the paper was completed. Other students will submit a "Sunday night special," hastily thrown together and proofread not by a careful parent but by the automated spell-checker on the computer. The differences between these two types of students were observed by the teacher at least 8 months earlier in the year, but nevertheless, all students operated under the same assignment system and thus the gulf between the first and second students persisted and perhaps widened. Teachers lament, "They've known about this for 2 months—they just didn't get organized." How could next year's assignment menu yield better results? The capstone term paper is worth 200 points for this teacher's assignments. In this class, 900 points earns a grade of A and 800 points earns a B, so a 200-point assignment represents a significant amount of work for the semester. How would results improve if the students' assignment instructed them to do the following?

Find a U.S. Supreme Court Opinion. Summarize the controversy, identify the parties, and state the Court's ruling. If there were dissenting opinions, explain the main issues on which the justices disagreed. (25 points. You may complete this assignment up to four times, for a total of 100 points.)

Identify a historical document that addresses an important historical controversy. The document could be a letter from a president or other leader, a proclamation, a political pamphlet, an annotated map, or other authentic historical document. Using the document and at least two other sources, such as histories or commentaries on the controversy, explain both sides of the controversy and the importance of the document in that controversy. (25 points. You may complete this assignment up to four times, for a total of 100 points.)

Each of these assignments is a bit more complicated than a typical piece of homework, but not nearly as overwhelming as a research paper. If students accumulate 200 points from these assignments, then they will be exempt from the requirement for the research paper. Note well that the students will—and this is the critical point—*still do as much work as if they had completed the research paper.* They will simply do that work in well-managed chunks and with more careful feedback from the teacher. Students do not learn to undertake major projects by failing to complete major projects; they learn to complete major projects by breaking those challenges down into smaller chunks and then executing each task.

The objections of critics are inevitable: Students who complete eight smaller assignments may have a good grasp of the essence of the learning expectations that the teacher had for the research paper, but they will not have expressed a unified and coherent argument within a single research paper. My response is that most high school research papers (and many in college as well) do not express a unified and coherent argument. Our task as teachers is to provide students with the building blocks for a complete research paper—analyzing an argument and reading complex and authentic material. Most importantly, teachers who use the menu system will have the opportunity to give incremental feedback throughout a 2-month period. If a student fails to follow instructions that are fairly clear and straightforward, then the consequence is not a failure but the requirement to respect the teacher's feedback and resubmit the work. This is a consequence that rarely occurs for "final" research papers. Moreover, it is a consequence that students loathe. I have heard them say "gimme the zero"—a consequence I find unacceptable. Eventually, they learn that the path of least resistance is to do the work correctly the first time. By giving students a rational choice, the quality of their work improves and the time allocation of the teacher is less frantic at the end of the year.

## Early Examinations

The final method for teachers to save time and gain greater focus is the use of early examinations. This is particularly helpful in those secondary school classes where final examinations may be required or, at the very least, are a cultural tradition. The following simple system was used in a midwestern ninth-grade science class in a school in which the schoolwide passing rate had been an unacceptably low 36%. The teachers began by agreeing on a consistent curriculum and providing common quarterly assessments. This helped, but their greatest innovation was the early final. Teachers created a second form of the final exam and offered it to students 2 weeks earlier than the regular final exam schedule. If, after the early final, students had earned an A or B in the class, then their semester was over for that class. They were not permitted to leave campus or otherwise get into trouble, but they would have 10 classroom days of freedom while their less successful colleagues were still cramming for finals. If, on the early final, students earned a C, D, or F, then they would receive very specific feedback from the teachers and could devote the final 10 days of class to focusing on their greatest learning needs. The results were striking: Passing rates increased from 36% to 69% after 1 year and to 92% after the second year. The students were the same—74% eligible for free or reduced-price lunch, high mobility, many speaking a language other than English—and so were the teachers. The changes were in practice and result, with teachers focusing on feedback and students focusing on performance. In the past, the final exam represented the ultimate judgment, with teacher as adjudicator and executioner. Now, the final exam was not final, and the role of the teacher changed dramatically from judge to coach. The consequent reduction in failure rate not only helped students, but it also dramatically improved the working conditions of teachers, with improved discipline, climate, and morale.

## Conclusion

If schools are to achieve focus, policy directives and administrative announcements are not enough. The demands on time are unending— each year there are more demands than time available. With more time, teachers can provide better feedback, build relationships, collaborate with their colleagues, develop improved assessments, and implement more deeply the instructional practices they have already learned. While the ideas in this chapter are not exhaustive, they offer a start for schools that are serious about focusing on what matters most. Certainly every reader can think of a reason that one or another strategy will fail. It is easy to imagine a student for whom a particular strategy will be futile, or to imagine an administrator who will resist any changes that lead to savings in time, but who nevertheless insists on the fantasy that everything will be accomplished if only the teachers work with sufficient zeal. But the comparison we must make is not between the ideas in this book and a fanciful ideal. The comparison is between the improvements offered in these pages and our present reality. In the vast majority of schools I have observed, that reality cries for improvement, and improvement of any sort—teaching, curriculum, or culture—begins with finding your leadership focus.

## CHAPTER 9

# Assessing and Sustaining Your Leadership Focus

NO EDUCATIONAL LEADER seeks a life that is overwhelmed, exhausted, and fragmented. The path toward initiative fatigue is paved with good intentions, commitments sincerely made, and the unflappable optimism that characterized leaders when they first aspired to a position of influence. The dark reality, however, is that neither good intentions nor sincerity is an adequate substitute for effective leadership focus. In this chapter, I will address how to assess leadership focus and, most importantly, how to sustain it. In her important book *Rapt*, Winifred Gallagher (2009) explores the power of personal and organizational focus. Exploding the myth of multitasking, she offers compelling evidence of the benefits of leading a focused life. In previous chapters, I have concentrated on the benefits of focus in terms of student achievement and organizational results. However, it is important not to neglect the profound personal benefits—including psychological, emotional, and physical health—that accrue from choosing focus over chaos.

If we know the value of focus and are equipped with the tools to achieve it, why is it so rare? Why do pilots ignore safety warnings and policies that require a focus on safety, and thus jeopardize the lives of their passengers? Why do train conductors send text messages, ignoring the stopped car in front of them? Focus saves lives and a lack of focus is deadly. School leaders know intellectually the power of focus, yet every year brings a proliferation of new initiatives but not the organizational discipline of removing unnecessary and conflicting initiatives. In the hours before writing this paragraph, I heard a superintendent claim to be focused exclusively on six priorities. Within minutes of that claim, however, I was treated to his proposed new "scorecard" that included

more than 100 initiatives, many of which were labels without meaningful explanations. His staff development catalog included more than 300
separate courses, some of which were more than a decade old and few
of which were linked clearly to the six priorities. The first two policy
documents I reviewed for this individual were laborious in their detail
and directly contradicted the provisions of the scorecard and the advice
of some of the staff development programs. This kind of situation is
pervasive in education. We talk a good game about focus, but the reality
is proliferation of programs and the accompanying fragmentation of the
time, attention, and emotional energy of leaders and teachers.

What power is so compelling that people forfeit common sense,
professional duty, and even their own lives, rather than follow the discipline of focus? Before becoming too judgmental about the failure of
others to focus, consider the results of the Leadership Focus Assessment
in Figure 9.1. Perhaps you will find, as I did, that it is much easier to
preach the virtues of focus than to practice them. Nevertheless, there
is hope. You can use this chapter to create a baseline measurement of
your own level of focus and hold yourself and your colleagues account-
able for visible improvements. Sustaining leadership focus is not an
event, decision, or policy prescription. It is a discipline, not unlike a
commitment to personal fitness. Running a marathon once a year may
represent a reasonable commitment to an attainable goal if it is accompanied by disciplined practice and preparation. But the same 26.2 miles
will ruin the joints, circulatory system, and psyche of the person who
fails to prepare for the challenge. Similarly, leadership focus requires
vigilance and attention, as well as an appreciation of irony. The latter
will be necessary when you hear someone say, "I just finished the latest
book by Doug Reeves and I'd like to announce a new initiative on leadership focus."

## The Leadership Focus Assessment

Figure 9.1 provides an instrument you can use to assess your level of
focus. This assessment will be most useful if you ask two or three people
close to you—including a colleague, administrative assistant, and family
member—to also complete the assessment with their candid observations
of your performance. This is not a search for numerical precision, so you

**FIGURE 9.1** The Leadership Focus Assessment

*Instructions:* Please respond to each statement with your level of agreement and a brief comment explaining your response. You will have the most meaningful results if you also ask a colleague, assistant, and family member to complete this assessment with their candid views of your performance.

1. When I assess the performance of the people who report directly to me, I have clear scoring guides (or rubrics) that help me communicate with my colleagues exactly what their performance levels are now and how their performance can improve.

   Strongly Agree    Agree    No Opinion    Disagree    Strongly Disagree

   Comments:

2. Within the past 4 weeks, I have gathered specific performance measurement information for the two or three most important initiatives in our system.

   Strongly Agree    Agree    No Opinion    Disagree    Strongly Disagree

   Comments:

3. I can identify at least three specific initiatives that we have evaluated and terminated in the past 12 months.

   Strongly Agree    Agree    No Opinion    Disagree    Strongly Disagree

   Comments:

4. In the past 3 working days, I have been able to complete all of the "A" priorities on my task list.

   Strongly Agree    Agree    No Opinion    Disagree    Strongly Disagree

   Comments:

5. In the past month, I have hardly ever missed or been late to a family commitment.

   Strongly Agree    Agree    No Opinion    Disagree    Strongly Disagree

   Comments:

6. In the past month, when I was faced with a new priority, project, or task, I specifically identified an old priority, project, or task that I decided to eliminate.

Strongly Agree     Agree     No Opinion     Disagree     Strongly Disagree

Comments:

7. When I look at the agenda of my most recent important meetings (board, cabinet, faculty, department), I see visible evidence that the agenda is shorter and more focused than the agenda for the same meeting 2 years ago. [If you are not sure, please take a moment to check—count the agenda items and pages of documents.]

Strongly Agree     Agree     No Opinion     Disagree     Strongly Disagree

Comments:

8. Within the past 24 hours, I have taken time to express personal and specific appreciation to a colleague using a personal note, voice-to-voice call, or personal meeting.

Strongly Agree     Agree     No Opinion     Disagree     Strongly Disagree

Comments:

9. Based on clear and convincing evidence available to me right now, I am certain that my actions and decisions influence student achievement.

Strongly Agree     Agree     No Opinion     Disagree     Strongly Disagree

Comments:

10. Since the time I started responding to this assessment a few minutes ago, I have not interrupted myself to respond to an e-mail, instant message, Tweet, text message, or any other electronic intrusion.

Strongly Agree     Agree     No Opinion     Disagree     Strongly Disagree

Comments:

*Scoring:* First, consider the responses of your colleague, assistant, and family member and make any necessary revisions in the responses above. Then, score 1 point for Strongly Agree, 2 points for Agree, 3 points for No Opinion, 4 points for Disagree, and 5 points for Strongly Disagree.

**My total Leadership Focus score:** _____

This figure is available for free download and printing from www.tcpress.com.

can consider the average of their responses if you wish. A better approach, however, might be to use the mode—the most frequent response—rather than the average. In other words, if you mark "agree" and your assistant, colleague, and spouse mark "strongly disagree," then don't kid yourself with the use of something between those two marks. They are speaking the truth, and you are fortunate indeed to have people who care about you enough to give you candid feedback.

## Scoring Your Leadership Focus Assessment

**40–50**   There is a clinical diagnosis for leaders like you—we call it "normal"—so quit beating yourself around the head and shoulders and let's work on this—perhaps even focus on it. You're already racked with guilt for being late to dinner with your spouse (again) or for forgetting your kid's little league game (the only home run he hit all year), and you can tell that your colleagues are near the breaking point not because they are incapable, but because all of you are so dedicated that you never decline a single request for assistance. You'll continue this behavior right up until the point when you are carried out of your office in a pine box, suffer a staff revolt, are served with divorce papers, or are—without seeing it coming—fired. These calamities happen to good people every day, and many of them thought that they could just work their way out of their troubles. There are many drugs available today that will provide a short-term boost to your mood. An addiction to frantic work is like carrying a syringe of adrenaline in your pocket. If that drug is more pleasurable for you than your health, family, and job, then don't worry about focus—everything must be working out well for you.

**30–39**   You're not over the edge, but you can see the precipice from where you're standing and the ground appears to be shifting downward, carrying you toward the cliff. It's not too late to change, but you've probably seen the warning signs before and ignored them. In fact, you've actually been recognized, rewarded, and promoted for ignoring the warning signs. Why change now? Become just a little less focused and you can enjoy the personal and professional success of your colleagues who scored over 40. After all, we all know that high scores are the name of the game in education.

**LESS THAN 30**  Remember the instructions about asking a colleague, assistant, and family member to take this assessment? Please go back and do that, as it is at least possible that friends and family will have a different perception of your focus than you do.

**IF I DID NOT THINK** that leadership focus was possible, I would not have conducted this research or written the book. But it is fair to say that both institutional and personal momentum militate against focus. If you can move yourself and your staff from a score of 50 to 40, from 45 to 35, from 40 to 30, you will literally save lives, relationships, and careers. You won't avoid unexpected diversions, unreasonable demands, and unsustainable initiatives, but you will improve your leadership focus.

## Sustaining Leadership Focus

Earlier in this book I issued a clarion call to "weed the garden," and that is how I will conclude. Weeds have deep roots and remarkable abilities to be impervious to the efforts of even the most diligent gardener. Moreover, many contemporary educational conferences and trends tend, shall we say, to offer abundant fertilizer for weeds. Breathtaking enthusiasm and groundless claims overtake descriptive clarity and evidentiary rigor. The fact-free debate leaves skeptics cast as uncooperative recalcitrants rather than professionals who know that any new initiative must be able to withstand challenges for improved clarity, replicable research, and practical application. I conclude the case for leadership focus with the following four guidelines for sustaining the journey.

First, buy two new in-boxes—one small and the other large. The first is for those items you can control and the second is for items you cannot control. The small in-box is slight of build and contains the documents, messages, and imperatives on which you will focus today. The large in-box is about the size of the Grand Canyon, and it contains the documents, reports, complaints, and messages that will be there for your successor and were probably there when your Paleolithic predecessor occupied your chair. I actually asked a carpenter friend of mine to build an enormous in-box—it's dark-stained walnut with sides that are about 8 inches high. I peer into its abyss about once every week or two, empty the contents into the trash, and then return to the small in-box.

Second, channel skepticism in the right direction. Many educational systems are divided into True Believers and Apostates. True Believers get it, Apostates don't. What would happen if we recast the "us versus them" contest of True Believers versus Apostates into constructive contention? Leaders would greet each new initiative not with unbridled enthusiasm, but with a genuine appeal to the critical thinking and problem-solving abilities of the staff. "I've heard a lot about this and even read a couple of books about it, but I want to be sure we do it right. So I'd like to ask Ms. Jenkins, Dr. Eicher, and Mr. Meek to prepare some critical questions for our next meeting. Ask the tough ones, think about what could go wrong, and help us anticipate challenges." Never mind that Jenkins, Eicher, and Meek were already busy preparing their critical inquiries for the faux faculty meeting that typically occurs in the parking lot. Now they have official sanction to do what they were going to do anyway— be critical and skeptical. Channel that intellectual energy in the right direction. Skeptics have a tough life but can nevertheless make important contributions to our work.

Third, commit to a culture of hypothesis testing. You will have passed this test when you can stand before your colleagues and say with complete authenticity, "Last year I had the following hypothesis about teaching, leadership, and learning and let me share with you how wrong I was." In my career as a researcher, I have been required to do this, and although it is a thoroughly humiliating exercise, it is a necessary one. We must be mindful of the admonition of educational philosopher Mark Twain, who remarked, "It ain't what you don't know that gets you into trouble. It's what you know for sure that just ain't so." There are many contemporary assertions about brain research, differentiated instruction, learning styles, instructional leadership, and a host of other issues. Some of these assertions will be supported by evidence and others will not. The latter is not a mark of intellectual failure of those who proposed the hypotheses, but rather a reflection that science marches on. Aristotle was a smart enough fellow, but today we know that there are more than four elements. Elizabeth the First may have much to teach about leadership and inspiration, but torture is not nice in either the 16th or the 21st century. Icons of educational research, from Edward L. Thorndike and Charles Spearman to the luminaries of the present day, have much to teach us, but they are not infallible. A culture of hypothesis testing reflects a commitment to the ideal that the lowliest monk can challenge the mightiest pope, and the quiet teacher-researcher can say without fear of retribution, "I've compared the claims of this theory to the reality of the classroom, and the theory is not sustainable."

Fourth, and most importantly, replace the "bias for action" (Peters & Waterman, 1982) that has dominated leadership thinking of the past three decades with a bias for discernment. Educational leaders have been too often seduced by strategic planning (or, more precisely, by those claiming to be strategic planners), and the results are fragmentation rather than focus. The bias for action leads to endless to-do lists; the bias for discernment leads to daily priorities linked explicitly to system goals. The bias for action leads to endless document production and deforestation; the bias for discernment is green in every sense of the word, not only relieving staff members of yet another three-ring binder full of impossible objectives but also providing a "go" signal for the most important actions of teachers and educational leaders.

The late Charles Schulz, creator of the iconic Peanuts comic strip, gave us the pleasure of starting every Sunday morning for 50 years with his wit and wisdom. One of his characters, Pig-Pen, was nearly invisible because he was always surrounded by a cloud of dust and debris. He was always moving, though one could not always tell in what direction. The image is a powerful one, not only because the cloud surrounding too many leaders is one of disarray, but also because these leaders carry elaborate planners. We want to tell them, "Stop! Slow down. Ditch the planner with the 78 strategic priorities! Just stop, breathe, and focus. You're a good person, but you're going to kill yourself and your staff with another year of frantic pursuit of multiple priorities."

Before *you* plan another year of conflicting priorities, projects, and action plans, please stop. Find your leadership focus.

# The Research in Depth

THE PURPOSE of this report was to determine the association between Planning, Implementation, and Monitoring (PIM™) rubric evaluation scores and student achievement, and to ascertain the way in which PIM scores function in clusters as they relate to student achievement. Specifically, the research attempted to answer four questions:

1. Which PIM characteristics combine to have the greatest impact on student achievement in all schools?
2. Which PIM characteristics are most associated with student achievement in high-poverty schools?
3. Which PIM characteristics are most associated with student achievement in low-poverty schools?
4. What is the relative impact of PIM characteristics and student demographics on individual achievement score gains and composite gains?

The PIM rubric is an instrument that uses ratings from 1 to 3, with 1 as a low score, 2 as a middle score, and 3 as a high score. For the purposes of this report, "High" PIM will be referred to as scores associated with 3, and "Low" PIM will be referred to as scores associated with 1. The rubric encompasses 15 variable indicators in three major groupings: planning, implementation, and monitoring. Hence, this study is predicated on the fact that leadership spends time on each of these 15 variables within a school year, which can be evidenced in their school improvement plans.

Because student achievement may be categorized based on specific student groupings, each of nine groups was analyzed for the way in which

PIM scores were related to student achievement. These groups include: All Schools, Elementary Schools, Middle Schools, High Schools, and schools with High PIM, Middle PIM, Low PIM, High Poverty, and High ESL (English as a second language). Alternative schools could not be included in the student achievement analyses because there were fewer than 20 of these schools with available student achievement data. Periods of achievement within the included groups were determined by 1- and 2-year student achievement gains by each school over a period of 3 years. For all schools in Canada and the United States, at least three tests were given in reading, writing, and math. Schools in the United States administered additional tests in science, as well as tests in reading, writing, math, science, and social studies in different grades.

## Terminology

In the study documents, the term "inquiry" refers to a question that reveals the beliefs of the leadership and teaching team about the causes of student achievement. When leaders and teachers have a high degree of efficacy, then their score in inquiry is high, reflecting the attitude by leaders and teachers that they are the primary sources of influence on student achievement. Low scores on this variable reflect the attitude by the leaders and teachers that the characteristics of students, rather than the actions of educational professionals, are the primary influences on student achievement. The term "inquiry" in the tables that follow is a measurement of efficacy as discussed in the main text of this book.

## Methodology

To determine the relationship between clusters of PIM scores and student achievement, factor analyses were used to discover which PIM variables could be combined for each grouping of indicators for each student group. Cluster sampling was then used to determine relative patterns in PIM scores across the 15 variable indicators. For those combined PIM scores, a scale, or sum of the variables, was used to replace the combined indicators. This was accomplished by using high loading factor analysis results for each variable and by selecting other variables for coupling procedures. To determine whether clusters of PIM scores, or combined variables, were related to student achievement, factor cluster scales were first produced, all scores were then sorted by PIM score scale values, then each grouping (High PIM and Low PIM) was measured using a *t*-test for independent samples. This test was used to determine whether High PIM scores were significantly higher or lower than Low PIM scores using a two-tailed test, or a test that checks for both increases and decreases in scores. The rationale for this approach was that if High PIM scores were significantly different from Low PIM scores, the difference would validate the association of the score values. In other words, High and Low PIM scores would be associated with high and low achievement.

To determine the relative impact of PIM scores on student achievement gains, factor analyses and multiple linear regressions were used. Factor analysis is a test that seeks to combine large numbers of variables, in this case 15 indicators, to reduce the repetition of unnecessary, often called redundant, variables. In this case, factor analysis was used to discover which PIM indicators could be combined so that cluster scales could be produced. In these scales, variables that loaded high on the factor analyses were summed. This process was also used to form factors (combined variables) so that regression analyses could determine whether or not the factors were directly related to student achievement. To maximize possible combinations of variables, factor loading standards were set at, or very close to, 0.7, which is usually used as the confirmatory, rather than exploratory, standard. Because this is a foundational study, maximized variable combinations were warranted. Multiple linear regressions use multiple correlations to find out how many independent variables, in this case the 15 PIM indicators, are related to a dependent variable, or one criterion. Both tests were used in combination to determine the relative impact of the indicators on student achievement.

## Discussion and Conclusions

The following discussion and conclusions are organized around the four original research questions.

### 1. Which PIM characteristics combine to have the greatest impact on student achievement in all schools?

One particular focus of this study was to examine how clusters of PIM variables related to student achievement, and the findings revealed three places in student demographics that show such combinations in the multivariate results. The first occurs in Math 2005, in which Inquiry Process and Specific Goals combine on Factor 1. Because these indicators by themselves show means of 2.51 and 2.54, the second and third highest means in 2005 for all available schools with demographics, and because they are significantly and inversely related to student achievement, leadership may want to spend less time on these goals when student achievement in Math is a focus.

The second combination occurs in schools with high ESL populations and relates to Science tests for 2006. The combination of Professional Development Emphasis and Monitoring Plan show significant and positive relationships to 2-year gains in Science. Because these indicators are lower in terms of their rank in the summary statistics, and because the standardized coefficient for this combination makes up almost ½ of a standard deviation as a beta statistic (.475), leadership should focus more time on these variables when Science is a focus for ESL students.

The last combination of this type is evidenced in schools with high special education populations (as indicated by the variable IEP [Individualized Education Plan]) for Science 2006. The combination of Master Plan Design, Professional Development Emphasis, and Professional Development Implementation, which form Factor 2 in this regression model, shows significant inverse relationships to student achievement on 2-year gains in Science. Because these three variables have Middle PIM scores, the data suggest that leadership may not be getting the biggest "bang for the buck" in these areas when the objective is increasing special education student achievement in Science.

#### Reading Achievement

In the bivariate analyses, the most significant pattern of PIM combinations occurs in Reading achievement gains for three groupings of variable indicators. In fact, for all schools without grade level groupings (e.g., high school, middle school, elementary school), Reading achievement is the only subject test indicating positive student achievement when grouping PIM variables for 1-year gains. The highest PIM grouping gain is evidenced when Inquiry Process, Monitoring Plan, Monitoring Frequency, and Evaluation Cycle are combined, producing Reading achievement increases of 145%, or a 2.4 gain, which is significant ($t = 3.1$, $p = .001$).

The other two groupings affecting Reading achievement are Specific Goals, Achievable Goals, and Master Plan, with an increase of 138%, also a 2.4 gain ($t = 3.11$, $p = .002$), and Professional Development Emphasis, Professional Development Implementation, and Monitoring Plan, with a 91% increase in Reading achievement, almost twice the difference between High and Low PIM scales.

In the multivariate analyses, factor analyses for 2005 and 2006 show high loadings, with Inquiry Process and Specific Goals on Factor 1 and Inquiry Process, Specific Goals, and Achievable Goals on Factor 2 for 2006. Professional Development Emphasis is also part of Factor 2 in 2005. For Reading achievement, Factor 1 (Inquiry Process and Specific Goals) shows a significant negative relationship with Reading. The standardized coefficient shows ¼ of a standard deviation in the negative, suggesting that time spent on Inquiry Process and Specific Goals combined (scale mean = 5.038) may not have an impact on student achievement in Reading.

### Math Achievement

Bivariate analyses show significant inverse relationships to Math achievement for all variable combinations: 95% to over 200% decreases in achievement based on significant PIM combinations. Multivariate analyses corroborate these findings, with the exception of Comprehensive Needs Assessment.

Comprehensive Needs Assessment shows a significant positive relationship to student achievement in Math for 2006, yet it has the lowest mean (1.082) of the 15 PIM indicators. The standardized coefficient is ⅛ of a standard deviation. Both Relevant Goals and Monitoring Frequency indicate significant inverse relationships, with standardized coefficients less than ⅕ of a standard deviation in the negative.

### Writing, Science, and All Tests Achievement

Bivariate analyses show one inverse relationship when combining Inquiry Process, Monitoring Plan, Monitoring Frequency, and Evaluation

Cycle. None of the factors is significant; however, Monitoring Plan shows a significant inverse relationship to Writing achievement, and Parental Involvement Strategies shows the only significant positive relationship, with the standardized coefficient showing just under ⅕ of a standard deviation, with a slope of 2.5, in relationship to student achievement in Writing.

Bivariate analyses show negligible relationships to student achievement. Aggregate test results indicate no statistically significant relationships to student achievement in multivariate analyses. Detailed data are available at The Leadership and Learning Center website: www.LeadandLearn.com.

## 2. Which PIM characteristics are most associated with student achievement in High-Poverty schools?

Perhaps the most interesting part of this study concerns High-Poverty student achievement as it relates to PIM variables. In bivariate analyses, the combination of six variables (Inquiry Process, Specific Goals, Achievable Goals, Relevant Goals, Parental Involvement Strategies, and Evaluation Cycle) showed a statistically significant increase of 208%, or a 3.1 gain, when comparing High PIM scores with Low PIM scores in Math for 2007.

The most consistent pattern in this category involves Professional Development Implementation in High-Poverty schools. For both 2005 and 2006, this indicator showed statistically significant positive relationships. These were both significant, at the .05 level and the .01 level, respectively. The slopes in order include: 7.553 for 2-year gains in Reading 2005, 9.170 for 2-year gains in Math 2005, and 24.622 for All Tests 2005. Because the mean for this indicator in 2005 is 1.4, the second lowest of all indicators, leadership should spend more time on this indicator to increase student achievement in High-Poverty schools.

The same variable, Professional Development Implementation, shows significantly inverse relationships with 2-year gains in Math 2006 and All Tests 2006, both significant at the .05 level. For Writing 2005, the relationship is also significantly inverse, as is the relationship for Targeted Research-Based Strategies.

For High-Poverty schools, the first combination of PIM variables of significance is Factor 1. Factor 1, the combination of Measurable Goals and Achievable Goals, is significantly and negatively related to student achievement in Writing for 2006 at the .05 level. This suggests that leadership may need to spend less time on these combined variables when Writing is a focus of student achievement in School Improvement Plans.

### 3. Which PIM characteristics are most associated with student achievement in Low-Poverty schools?

There were no statistically significant combinations of PIM variables for Low-Poverty schools. However, Monitoring Plan evidenced a significant inverse relationship for 2-year gains in Writing achievement for 2005, at the .05 level.

### 4. What is the relative impact of PIM characteristics and student demographics on individual achievement score gains and composite gains?

#### High ESL Rates
In bivariate analyses, schools with High ESL rates, indicated by limited English proficiency (LEP), showed statistically significant inverse relationships when High PIM scores were compared with Low PIM scores, with Professional Development Implementation and Parental Involvement Strategies combined as a cluster for 1-year gains for All Tests 2007.

In multivariate analyses, schools with High ESL populations showed a significant inverse relationship to 2-year gains in Math achievement in 2005 and 2006, both significant at the .01 level. Conversely, significant positive relationships were evidenced in Writing for 2005 and 2006, both significant at the .05 level.

Inquiry Process showed significant inverse relationships to 2-year gains in All Tests 2006 and in Science 2006, which were both significant at the .05 level. Also, for All Tests 2006, Measurable Goals showed a significant inverse relationship to 2-year gains, while Targeted Research-Based Strategies showed a significant positive relationship to 2-year gains in Science 2006, significant at the .05 level. The slope for this variable is 8.4, and the standardized coefficient is .52, more than ½ of a standard deviation. Thus, leadership should spend more time on research-based strategies when focusing on student achievement for High ESL populations in Science. Master Plan Design also showed a significant inverse relationship to 2-year gains in Science 2006.

### High Special Education Populations (IEP)

This variable was not part of the original study, and it will not be found in the bivariate analyses. However, the data revealed some interesting relationships in the multivariate results to 2-year gains for one particular indicator in three areas, forming an emergent pattern. As mentioned earlier, this population also yielded a significant inverse relationship when three PIM variables were combined.

Master Plan Design showed a significant positive relationship to 2-year gains for All Tests, Math, and Science in 2006, all significant at >.01. The standardized coefficients for each occurrence are between .35 and .48. Leadership with a focus on students with special needs should spend more time on this variable to impact overall student achievement for students with IEPs, particularly in Math and Science.

Parental Involvement Strategies also showed a significant inverse relationship to 2-year gains in Reading for 2005, significant at the .05 level.

### Ethnicity Comparisons

Because the variable White showed collinearity (a very high correlation) with other variables, that population is not part of this discussion. However, the populations of Asian, Black, and Hispanic students showed consistent patterns in terms of relationships to 2-year gains.

#### Asian American Students

For Reading 2005 and 2006, as well as All Tests 2005, students identified by the variable Asian showed significant inverse relationships for 2-year gains in achievement. However, the slopes were less than 1.0 in all three cases, and standardized coefficients are less than ⅕ of a standard deviation in the negative.

#### African American Students

Students identified by the variable Black showed significant positive relationships for 2-year gains in Reading 2005 and 2006, as well as in Writing 2006 and All Tests 2005. The slopes ranged from .137 to .378, with standardized coefficients from .17 to .19.

*Hispanic American Students*

Students identified by the variable Hispanic showed significant positive relationships for 2-year gains in Reading 2005 and 2006 and in Math 2005 and 2006. The standardized coefficients for this group were relatively high, ranging from .632 to .844.

# The Nonlinear, Noninternal Nature of
# Student Achievement Variables

There is a fundamental flaw in the application of statistical analysis to variables involving student achievement, teaching, and leadership. While the statistical methods most commonly employed contain implicit assumptions about even intervals between data points and linear relationships among variables, the truth is that these assumptions are not accurate for most measurements of student achievement and human behavior. Therefore, it is not accurate to rank order impact or to presume the precision that statistical analysis often implies. From a practitioner's perspective, the best that we can say is that these data suggest that, after repeated analysis, focus on some variables is more consistently associated with gains in achievement than focus on other variables. Moreover, we can infer that some of these variables are context-dependent, showing different magnitudes of impact depending on the characteristics of the student population. This does not yield silver bullets, but only steps up the ladder of inference.

In the end, my purpose is neither to claim to settle the issue of school leadership nor to be so self-deprecating that this research is dismissed, but only to be as candid as possible about the strengths and limitations of the work.

# Descriptive Histograms

## *Analysis by School Type*

The histograms in Figures A.1–A.4 include all schools with PIM data for 2006–2007.

In Figure A.1, the histogram for all schools combined, the greatest frequency of PIM scores of 1 (Low PIM) occurs at the "bookends" of Comprehensive Needs Assessment and Evaluation Cycle, while the highest PIM scores (3) occur in Inquiry Process, several of the Goals (Achievable Goals as the highest), and Parental Involvement Strategies.

In Figure A.2, the histogram for elementary schools, the same pattern is prevalent, with Comprehensive Needs Assessment and Evaluation Cycle having the highest frequency of Low PIM scores, and Achievable Goals and Parental Involvement Strategies providing the greatest numbers of High PIM scores.

In Figure A.3, the histogram for middle schools, the same pattern is evident, with the lowest PIM scores in Comprehensive Needs Assessment and Evaluation Cycle, and the highest PIM scores in Achievable Goals (with the highest PIM) and Specific Goals.

Figure A.4 shows the histogram for all high schools. As in Figures A.1–A.3, Comprehensive Needs Assessment and Evaluation Cycle demonstrate the very highest frequencies of Low PIM scores. While Achievable Goals shows the greatest occurrence of High PIM scores (33%), this result is outweighed by the Low PIM values (52%), the same pattern that exists in Figures A.1–A.3.

**FIGURE A.1**   Histogram of All Schools: Frequency Percentage for PIM, 2006–2007 ($n$ = 863)

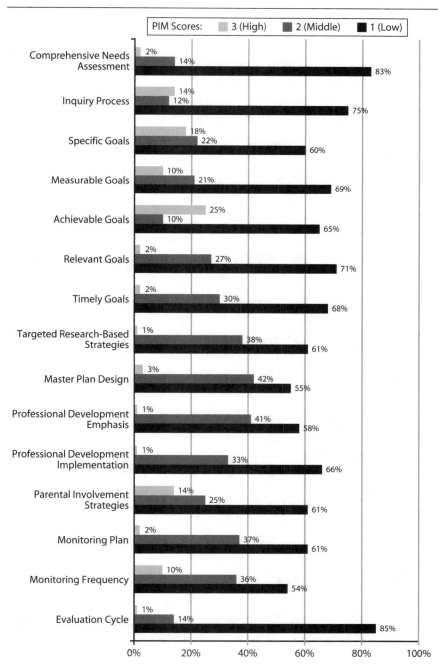

**FIGURE A.2**  Histogram of All Elementary Schools: Frequency Percentage for PIM, 2006–2007 (*n* = 648)

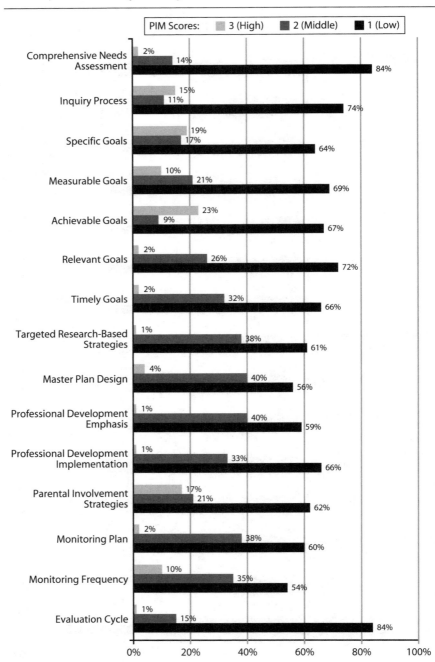

**FIGURE A.3**  Histogram of All Middle Schools: Frequency Percentage for PIM, 2006–2007 (*n* = 135)

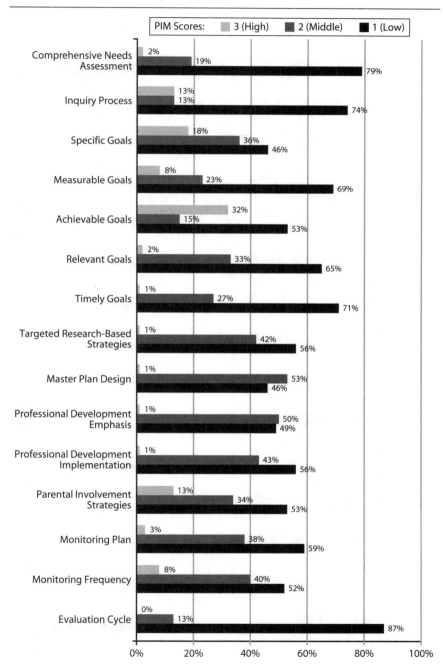

**FIGURE A.4**  Histogram of All High Schools: Frequency Percentage for PIM, 2006–2007 ($n = 97$)

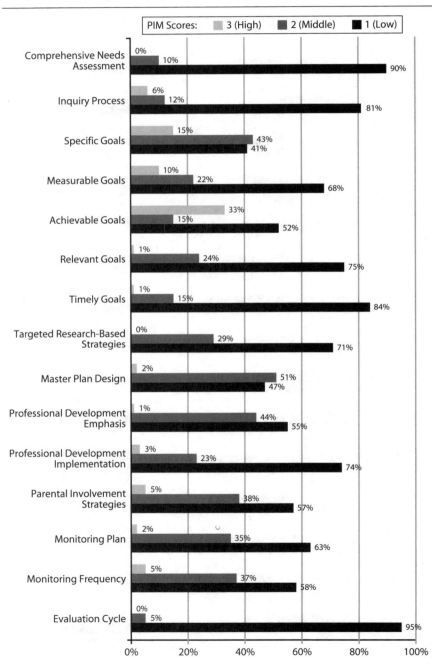

## Analysis by Total PIM Rubric Score

The histograms in Figures A.5–A.7 represent High, Middle, and Low Total PIM Rubric Scores for all schools combined, as determined by the total rubric sum for each school. Based on the frequency distribution of the total rubric scores, 37% of the schools were grouped as Low Total PIM Rubric Score (rubric sums of 15–17), 29% were grouped as Middle Total PIM Rubric Score (rubric sums of 18–22), and 34% were grouped as High Total PIM Rubric Score (rubric sums of 23–38). (*Note:* The maximum possible total rubric sum for the 15 evaluated variables is 45.)

In Figure A.5, the histogram for schools with High Total PIM Rubric Scores, the pattern of Low PIM for Comprehensive Needs Assessment and Evaluation Cycle seen in Figures A.1–A.4 is still evident, although to much lesser extent. Achievable Goals again shows the highest overall frequency of High PIM, but without the contrasting lower PIM frequencies seen in previous histograms. Moreover, Specific Goals and Inquiry Process, along with Parental Involvement Strategies and Monitoring Frequency, show higher percentages of High PIM than is seen in the previous histograms.

In Figure A.6, the histogram for schools with Middle Total PIM Rubric Scores, although Comprehensive Needs Assessment and Evaluation Cycle show much the same pattern as previous histograms with respect to PIM scores of 1 (Low PIM), Inquiry Process and Relevant Goals show slightly higher frequencies of Low PIM scores. Among the very few PIM scores above 2, only Measurable Goals shows a PIM score of 3 (High PIM) at more than single-digit frequency.

In Figure A.7, the histogram of Low Total PIM Rubric Score, schools with the lowest overall rubric sums show extremely high percentages of Low PIM scores. The only variable that shows a PIM rating of 3 (High PIM) is Measurable Goals, with a 2% frequency of that score. All ratings of 2 occur at frequencies below 15%. Among all PIM indicators, 94% have ratings of 1, or Low PIM scores.

**FIGURE A.5**   Histogram of High Total PIM Rubric Score, All Schools: Frequency Percentage for PIM, 2006–2007 ($n = 302$)

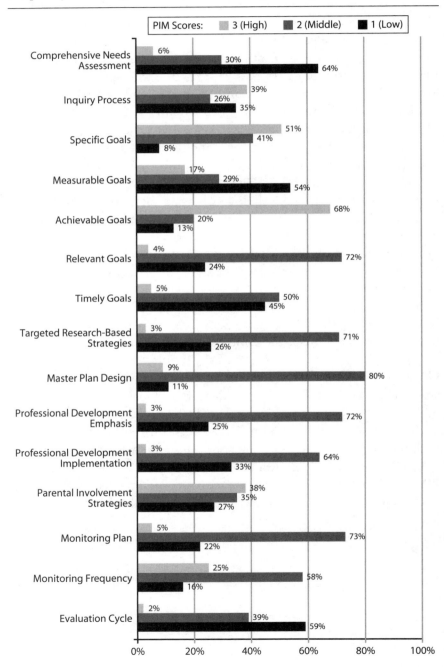

**FIGURE A.6** Histogram of Middle Total PIM Rubric Score, All Schools: Frequency Percentage for PIM, 2006–2007 ($n$ = 259)

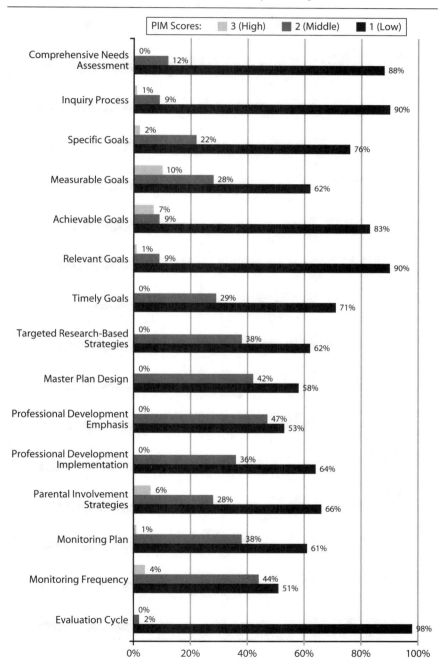

**FIGURE A.7**   Histogram of Low Total PIM Rubric Score, All Schools: Frequency Percentage for PIM, 2006–2007 ($n$ = 333)

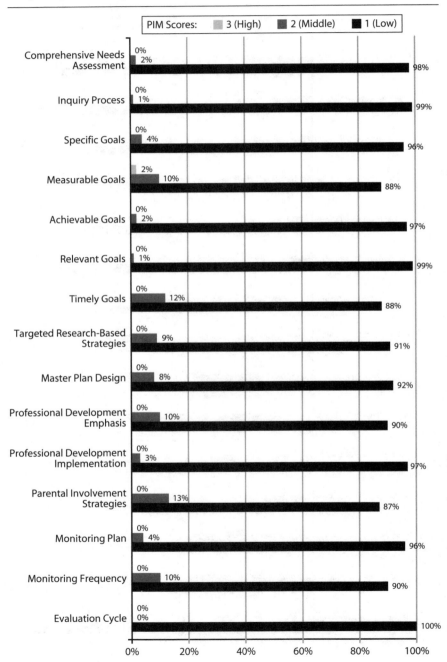

## Analysis by Student Demographics

Because this report was formulated based on existing information, the PIM groupings in Figures A.8–A.10 are limited to schools with available demographic data.

Figure A.8 shows the histogram for High Poverty, as indicated by >80% eligibility of students for free/reduced lunch. Although Comprehensive Needs Assessment and Evaluation Cycle show the typical pattern of high frequencies of Low PIM ratings of 1, the data indicate high frequencies of low ratings also for Measurable Goals (72%) and Timely Goals (62%). Achievable Goals shows the highest frequency of PIM 3 ratings (78%), followed by Specific Goals and Parental Involvement Strategies, both with 54% frequencies of PIM 3 ratings. Master Plan Design and Monitoring Plan indicators show unusually high frequencies of PIM ratings of 2.

In Figure A.9, the histogram of High ESL, the >45% LEP criterion was chosen because it represents the highest quartile of LEP among schools in the 2007 sample. In these data, Comprehensive Needs Assessment and Evaluation Cycle again show high frequencies of Low PIM scores, as do Measurable Goals and Timely Goals. The histogram also shows a high frequency of High PIM scores for Parental Involvement Strategies and Achievable Goals.

In Figure A.10, the histogram of High IEP, the >11% IEP criterion was chosen because it represents the highest quartile of IEP among schools in the 2007 sample. In these data, Comprehensive Needs Assessment and Evaluation Cycle show the highest frequencies of Low PIM scores, with Measurable Goals, Inquiry Process, and Timely Goals showing Low PIM scores to a lesser (but still high) extent. The highest PIM scores in this set are seen for Achievable Goals and Specific Goals.

**FIGURE A.8**   Histogram of High Poverty, as Indicated by Free/Reduced Lunch Eligibility Higher Than 80%, for PIM, 2006–2007 (*n* = 50)

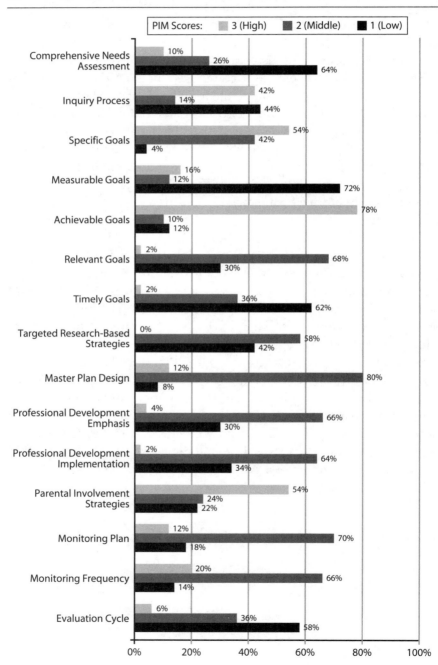

**FIGURE A.9**   Histogram of High ESL, as Indicated by LEP Higher Than 45%, for PIM, 2006–2007 ($n = 41$)

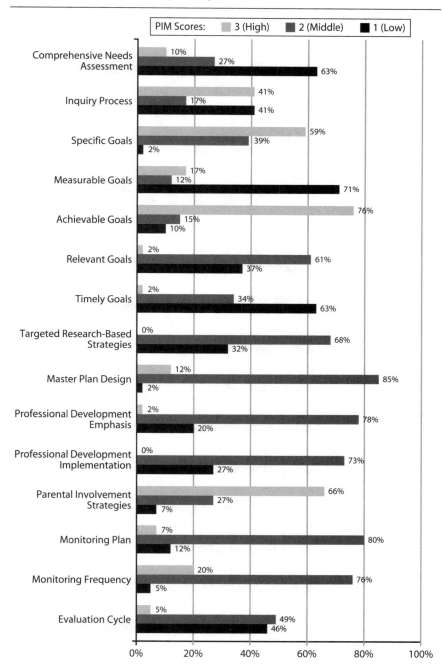

**FIGURE A.10**  Histogram of High IEP, as Indicated by IEP Higher Than
11%, for PIM, 2006–2007 (*n* = 120)

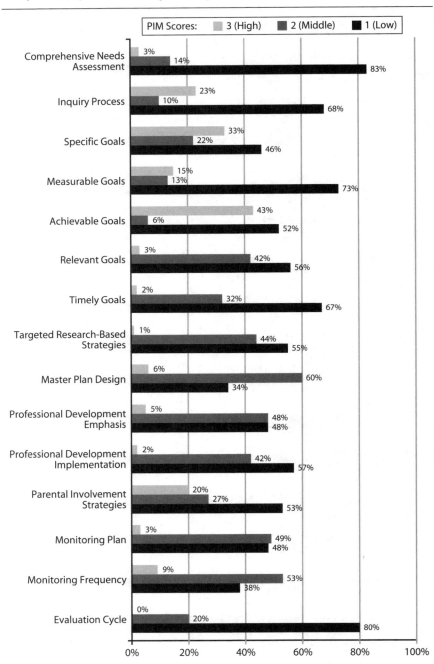

# Factor Analyses

The factor analyses given in Figures A.11–A.16 show the loadings for each indicator (variable). All loadings over 0.65 are highlighted (bold), indicating their combination into one factor. These tables are organized in the order of the original research questions: All Schools, High Poverty, and Low Poverty. A separate factor analysis is not provided for demographics, the last research question, because it is the same as the first question in this instance.

For all schools in 2005 (Figure A.11), variables with high factor loadings (0.65 and higher) on Factor 1 (F1) are Inquiry Process and Specific Goals, and variables with high loadings on Factor 2 (F2) are Targeted Research-Based Strategies and Professional Development Emphasis. In 2006 (Figure A.12), variables with high loadings on Factor 1 include Master Plan Design, Professional Development Emphasis, and Monitoring Plan. Variables with high loadings on Factor 2 are Inquiry Process, Specific Goals, and Achievable Goals.

For High-Poverty schools in 2005 (Figure A.13), variables with high loadings on Factor 1 are Relevant Goals, Master Plan Design, and Monitoring Plan, and variables loading high on Factor 2 are Specific Goals and Measurable Goals. In 2006 (Figure A.14), variables with high loadings on Factor 1 are Specific Goals, Measurable Goals, and Achievable Goals. Variables loading high on Factor 2 are Master Plan Design, Professional Development Emphasis, and Professional Development Implementation.

For Low-Poverty schools in 2005 (Figure A.15), variables with high loadings on Factor 1 are Inquiry Process, Specific Goals, Measurable Goals, and Achievable Goals, and variables loading high on Factor 2 are Timely Goals, Targeted Research-Based Strategies, and Professional Development Implementation. In 2006 (Figure A.16), variables with high loadings on Factor 1 are Master Plan Design, Professional Development Emphasis, Professional Development Implementation, Monitoring Plan, and Monitoring Frequency. Variables loading high on Factor 2 are Inquiry Process, Specific Goals, and Achievable Goals.

**FOR THE FULL SET OF TABLES** reporting this research, including results of multiple linear regressions with PIM combinations, see The Leadership and Learning Center website: www.LeadandLearn.com.

**FIGURE A.11**   Factor Analysis, All Schools, 2005

|  | F1 | F2 |
|---|---|---|
| 2005  Comprehensive Needs Assessment | 0.136 | 0.159 |
| **2005  Inquiry Process** | **0.908** | 0.122 |
| **2005  Specific Goals** | **0.695** | 0.083 |
| 2005  Measurable Goals | 0.565 | 0.225 |
| 2005  Achievable Goals | 0.581 | 0.097 |
| 2005  Relevant Goals | 0.445 | 0.130 |
| 2005  Timely Goals | 0.068 | 0.631 |
| **2005  Targeted Research-Based Strategies** | 0.151 | **0.672** |
| 2005  Master Plan Design | 0.245 | 0.625 |
| **2005  Professional Development Emphasis** | 0.170 | **0.680** |
| 2005  Professional Development Implementation | 0.151 | 0.647 |
| 2005  Parental Involvement Strategies | −0.045 | 0.161 |
| 2005  Monitoring Plan | 0.248 | 0.564 |
| 2005  Monitoring Frequency | 0.159 | 0.341 |
| 2005  Evaluation Cycle | 0.164 | 0.200 |

**FIGURE A.12**   Factor Analysis, All Schools, 2006

|  | F1 | F2 |
|---|---|---|
| 2006  Comprehensive Needs Assessment | 0.073 | 0.099 |
| **2006  Inquiry Process** | 0.040 | **0.733** |
| **2006  Specific Goals** | −0.009 | **0.942** |
| 2006  Measurable Goals | 0.122 | 0.492 |
| **2006  Achievable Goals** | 0.046 | **0.698** |
| 2006  Relevant Goals | 0.252 | 0.340 |
| 2006  Timely Goals | 0.242 | 0.099 |
| 2006  Targeted Research-Based Strategies | 0.378 | 0.372 |
| **2006  Master Plan Design** | **0.746** | 0.071 |
| **2006  Professional Development Emphasis** | **0.657** | −0.026 |
| 2006  Professional Development Implementation | 0.649 | −0.021 |
| 2006  Parental Involvement Strategies | 0.205 | 0.124 |
| **2006  Monitoring Plan** | **0.813** | 0.142 |
| 2006  Monitoring Frequency | 0.568 | 0.176 |
| 2006  Evaluation Cycle | 0.251 | 0.078 |

**FIGURE A.13**   Factor Analysis, High-Poverty Schools, 2005

|  | F1 | F2 |
|---|---|---|
| 2005  Comprehensive Needs Assessment | 0.201 | 0.503 |
| 2005  Inquiry Process | 0.355 | 0.475 |
| **2005  Specific Goals** | −0.030 | **0.801** |
| **2005  Measurable Goals** | −0.247 | **0.719** |
| 2005  Achievable Goals | −0.048 | 0.496 |
| **2005  Relevant Goals** | **0.796** | 0.082 |
| 2005  Timely Goals | 0.432 | −0.142 |
| 2005  Targeted Research-Based Strategies | 0.540 | 0.037 |
| **2005  Master Plan Design** | **0.728** | 0.310 |
| 2005  Professional Development Emphasis | 0.329 | 0.395 |
| 2005  Professional Development Implementation | 0.474 | 0.473 |
| 2005  Parental Involvement Strategies | −0.066 | 0.276 |
| **2005  Monitoring Plan** | **0.720** | 0.156 |
| 2005  Monitoring Frequency | 0.589 | −0.197 |
| 2005  Evaluation Cycle | 0.469 | −0.244 |

**FIGURE A.14**   Factor Analysis, High-Poverty Schools, 2006

|  | F1 | F2 |
|---|---|---|
| 2006  Comprehensive Needs Assessment | 0.042 | 0.131 |
| 2006  Inquiry Process | 0.570 | −0.008 |
| **2006  Specific Goals** | **0.659** | −0.104 |
| **2006  Measurable Goals** | **0.699** | 0.098 |
| **2006  Achievable Goals** | **0.767** | −0.029 |
| 2006  Relevant Goals | 0.299 | 0.263 |
| 2006  Timely Goals | −0.158 | 0.178 |
| 2006  Targeted Research-Based Strategies | 0.533 | 0.102 |
| **2006  Master Plan Design** | 0.070 | **0.755** |
| **2006  Professional Development Emphasis** | −0.250 | **0.822** |
| **2006  Professional Development Implementation** | −0.016 | **0.772** |
| 2006  Parental Involvement Strategies | 0.191 | 0.187 |
| 2006  Monitoring Plan | 0.259 | 0.638 |
| 2006  Monitoring Frequency | 0.569 | 0.536 |
| 2006  Evaluation Cycle | 0.437 | 0.272 |

**FIGURE A.15**   Factor Analysis, Low-Poverty Schools, 2005

|                                                      | F1     | F2     |
|------------------------------------------------------|--------|--------|
| 2005  Comprehensive Needs Assessment                 | 0.227  | −0.015 |
| **2005  Inquiry Process**                            | **0.837** | 0.282  |
| **2005  Specific Goals**                             | **0.801** | 0.172  |
| **2005  Measurable Goals**                           | **0.682** | 0.362  |
| **2005  Achievable Goals**                           | **0.726** | 0.252  |
| 2005  Relevant Goals                                 | 0.634  | −0.110 |
| **2005  Timely Goals**                               | 0.044  | **0.790** |
| **2005  Targeted Research-Based Strategies**         | 0.343  | **0.704** |
| 2005  Master Plan Design                             | 0.212  | 0.641  |
| 2005  Professional Development Emphasis              | 0.161  | 0.617  |
| **2005  Professional Development Implementation**    | 0.167  | **0.831** |
| 2005  Parental Involvement Strategies                | −0.100 | 0.295  |
| 2005  Monitoring Plan                                | 0.450  | 0.334  |
| 2005  Monitoring Frequency                           | 0.479  | 0.360  |
| 2005  Evaluation Cycle                               | 0.508  | 0.027  |

**FIGURE A.16**   Factor Analysis, Low-Poverty Schools, 2006

|                                                      | F1     | F2     |
|------------------------------------------------------|--------|--------|
| 2006  Comprehensive Needs Assessment                 | −0.003 | 0.395  |
| **2006  Inquiry Process**                            | 0.330  | **0.909** |
| **2006  Specific Goals**                             | 0.456  | **0.758** |
| 2006  Measurable Goals                               | 0.008  | 0.563  |
| **2006  Achievable Goals**                           | 0.127  | **0.672** |
| 2006  Relevant Goals                                 | 0.486  | 0.582  |
| 2006  Timely Goals                                   | 0.299  | 0.270  |
| 2006  Targeted Research-Based Strategies             | 0.644  | 0.368  |
| **2006  Master Plan Design**                         | **0.671** | 0.291  |
| **2006  Professional Development Emphasis**          | **0.680** | 0.012  |
| **2006  Professional Development Implementation**    | **0.815** | 0.165  |
| 2006  Parental Involvement Strategies                | 0.333  | 0.058  |
| **2006  Monitoring Plan**                            | **0.752** | 0.079  |
| **2006  Monitoring Frequency**                       | **0.741** | 0.034  |
| 2006  Evaluation Cycle                               | 0.259  | −0.270 |

# PIM™
# (Planning, Implementation, and Monitoring)
# School Improvement Audit

THE PIM™ (Planning, Implementation, and Monitoring) School Improvement Audit assesses levels of focus in 30 specific leadership practices in five broad areas:

- Comprehensive needs assessment
- Inquiry process
- SMART goals
- Design
- Evaluation

The rubric provides specific performance criteria for the leadership practices to facilitate assignment of PIM scores as follows:

- Score 3, exemplary performance (High PIM)
- Score 2, proficient performance (Middle PIM)
- Score 1, needs improvement (Low PIM)

The PIM™ School Improvement Audit thus provides an objective means of gathering and comparing data on a wide range of leadership practices from large numbers of schools with diverse student populations and operating in diverse environments.

This appendix is available for free download and printing from www.tcpress.com.

## Section A: Comprehensive Needs Assessment (5 practices)

| Exemplary: Score of 3 (all of 2 +) | Proficient: Score of 2 | Needs Improvement: Score of 1 |
|---|---|---|
| In addition to meeting requirements at the Proficient level, specific evidence is provided in needs assessment areas to describe: | Specific evidence is provided in needs assessment areas to describe: | Needs assessment areas provide any evidence to describe: |
| 1. Strengths are described specifically for student achievement, teaching practices, and leadership actions. | 1. Strengths are specified in more than just the student achievement area, identifying strengths of the staff and school. | 1. Strengths are limited to student achievement, and are vague or nonspecific regarding staff strengths. |
| 2. Student achievement is described in terms of state or district assessments, school-based assessments that describe subscale distinctions by subgroups, and classroom or contextual data that describe patterns and trends down to the skill level. | 2. Student achievement data include some evidence of school-level achievement data, narrative, and school/classroom data to support district or state assessment data. | 2. Data are primarily described in terms of standardized test scores or state-level assessments of student achievement, attendance, and demographics. |
| 3. Teacher practices are supported by research, describe whether professional development or repeated practice is needed, and describe how monitoring of those practices will be used to improve instruction. | 3. Teacher practices are supported by research and specific professional development needs. | 3. Teacher practices are generic statements that may identify strategies supported by research, but fail to link to specific need for professional development. |
| 4. Leadership actions describe the degree to which leaders monitor performance, set direction, provide feedback, or communicate values. | 4. Leadership actions describe the degree to which leaders specifically monitor performance or set direction. | 4. Leadership actions are not specifically distinguished from actions of other staff, or plan lacks clear description of actions. |

| Exemplary: Score of 3 (all of 2 +) | Proficient: Score of 2 | Needs Improvement: Score of 1 |
|---|---|---|
| 5. Evidence of frequent (beyond traditional grading periods) parent communication regarding standards, best practices, and grading (e.g., standards-based report card, Educational Testing Service [ETS], writing, etc.):<br>• Evidence of engagement of parents, patrons, and partner businesses or organizations is clearly described.<br>• Links readers to various data warehouses for demographic and student achievement data. | 5. One or more instances of involvement of parents in process of improving student achievement (e.g., online student monitoring, participation in curriculum design, methods to support learning at home). | 5. Compliance with P.L. 221 membership, and evidence of parent involvement tends to be in areas other than teaching and learning (e.g., % participation in conferences, attendance at school events, newsletters, assistance in school events). |

## Section B: Inquiry Process (4 practices)

| Exemplary: Score of 3 (all of 2 +) | Proficient: Score of 2 | Needs Improvement: Score of 1 |
|---|---|---|
| 6. Inquiry routinely examines cause-and-effect correlations from needs assessment data before selecting **ANY** strategies or program solutions. Positive correlations at desired levels represent a quantifiable vision of the future. | 6. Inquiry has identified some correlations from needs assessment data to select specific strategies or program solutions. Positive correlations at desired levels represent a quantifiable vision of the future. | 6. Effects (results targeted) may or may not align with urgent needs assessed or represent a quantifiable vision of the future. Plan tends to address broad content area improvement needs, without identified correlations between needs and strategies. |
| 7. **ALL** selected classroom-level research-based programs or instructional strategies are identified for a stated purpose, and **ALL** standards-based research strategies are designed to address **specific needs** in student achievement. | 7. Majority of selected classroom-level research-based programs or instructional strategies are identified for a **stated purpose**. Most schoolwide programs or strategies (e.g., NCLB research-based programs, collaborative scoring, dual-block algebra, tailored summer school) specify the **student needs** being addressed. | 7. Few (≤50%) classroom-level research-based instructional strategies. Few programmatic and structural antecedents identified on the basis of data supporting the need for that program or strategy. |

| Exemplary: Score of 3 (all of 2 +) | Proficient: Score of 2 | Needs Improvement: Score of 1 |
|---|---|---|
| 8. **Explicit evidence indicates routine data analysis to identify cause-and-effect correlations. ALL** causes are adult actions or the result of adult decisions rather than demographic student or family factors outside of the instructional control of educators. | 8. Most described causes are adult actions or the result of adult decisions rather than demographic student or family factors outside of the instructional control of educators; school improvement plan (SIP) describes some links between causes (antecedents) and desired results (effects). | 8. Evidence of analysis of cause-and-effect correlations is not described in the SIP. Causes either are absent or tend to be demographic factors outside of instructional control rather than adult actions and strategies. SIP rarely inquires regarding cause–effect relationships. |
| 9. **ALL** effects (desired results or goals) are specifically linked to cause behaviors or antecedent conditions for learning or administrative structures (e.g., time and opportunity, resources, etc.). | 9. Majority of effects (desired results or goals) are explicitly linked to identified causes, strategies, conditions for learning, or administrative structures. | 9. Few (≤50%) effects are explicitly linked to identified causes, strategies, conditions for learning, or administrative conditions. |

## Section C: SMART Goals (5 practices)

| Exemplary: Score of 3 (all of 2 +) | Proficient: Score of 2 | Needs Improvement: Score of 1 |
|---|---|---|
| 10. ALL Goals and supporting Targets **specify:**<br>• Targeted student groups,<br>• Grade level,<br>• Standard or content area and subskills that are delineated within that content area,<br>• Assessments specified to address subgroup needs. | 10. More than one Goal and supporting Target specify:<br>• Targeted student groups,<br>• Grade level,<br>• Standard or content area and subskills that are delineated within that content area,<br>• Assessments specified to address subgroup needs. | 10. Most Goals and supporting Targets describe in **general rather than specific terms:**<br>• Targeted student groups,<br>• Grade level,<br>• Standard or content area and subskills that are delineated within that content area. |

Specific

| | Measurable | Achievable | Relevant | Timely |
|---|---|---|---|---|
| (Level 1) | 11. ALL Goals/Targets describe: • Quantifiable measures of performance, • Baseline data are always provided for each Goal/Target. | 12. ALL Goals/Targets are sufficiently challenging to close learning gaps in 3–5 years for targeted subgroups. | 13. In addition to alignment of Goals/Targets with urgent student needs, ALL Goals can be explicitly linked to the mission and beliefs of the school or district. | 14. Each Goal and Target describes a fixed date when it will be achieved. |
| (Level 2) | 11. All Goals/Targets describe quantifiable measures of performance with specific assessments. | 12. At least one Goal/Target is sufficiently challenging to close learning gaps in 3–5 years for targeted subgroups. Learning gaps are specified. | 13. All Goals/Targets align with urgent student needs identified in comprehensive needs assessment (subgroups specified). Some Goals are explicitly linked to the mission or stated beliefs of the school or district. | 14. Some Goals/Targets describe a fixed date when they will be achieved, but all Goals/Targets specify a specific window of time. |
| (Level 3) | 11. Few Goals/Targets describe quantifiable measures of performance. Stated goals seldom reference student needs or growth targets or specific assessment tools. | 12. Goals/Targets are set so low that achievement will not close learning gaps in foreseeable future, or there are insufficient data to determine whether any learning gaps will be closed by achieving goal targets. | 13. Few Goals/Targets describe urgent student needs identified in comprehensive needs assessment. Links to mission or beliefs of the school or district are vague or absent. | 14. Goals/Targets rarely describe a fixed date when they will be achieved, and describe only broad windows of time for any Goals (seasons, years). |

Minimal Growth from Baseline to Close Gaps: 1st Quartile ≥10%; 2nd Quartile ≥10%; 3rd Quartile ≥5%; Highest Quartile ≥3%

## Section D: Design (11 practices)

| Exemplary: Score of 3 (all of 2 +) | Proficient: Score of 2 | Needs Improvement: Score of 1 |
|---|---|---|
| Design describes, in addition to all requirements of Proficient level: | Design describes: | Design describes: |
| 15. **WHY each** focus area or major action step is being implemented. | 15. **WHY** some action steps are implemented. SIP describes **HOW** the plan will be implemented, when, in what settings, and by whom. | 15. When plan will be implemented and by whom. |
| 16. **Multiple forms of student assessment data, including formative, as well as multiple measures of teacher practices and leader actions.** | 16. Multiple student achievement assessment data and some data for teacher practices targeted. | 16. Assessments are more often used to comply with directives rather than to serve as indicators of change or improved achievement. |
| 17. **Explicit evidence** of improvement cycles for **every school improvement initiative.** | 17. Explicit evidence of improvement cycles for some improvement initiatives. | 17. Evidence of improvement cycles for school wide initiatives unclear. |
| 18. Monitoring schedule (≥ monthly) that **reviews both student performance and adult teaching practices.** | 18. Monitoring schedule (≥ monthly) to review student performance. | 18. Monitoring less frequent than monthly for student performance or teaching practices. |
| 19. **Capacity for rapid rollout of team responses** (to data, professional development, coaching, adjusted time and opportunity) in response to needs. | 19. Some midcourse corrections delineated or anticipated in design of SIP. | 19. No description of midcourse corrections observed in SIP design. |
| 20. All Results Indicators serve as **interim progress probes** for each SMART Goal. | 20. Some Results Indicators serve as interim progress probes for SMART Goals. | 20. Results Indicators vague, describe compliance, or difficult to measure. |

| | | |
|---|---|---|
| 21. Consideration of **adult learning issues and the change process is evident** in time, programs, and resources. | 21. Some attention to adult learning issues and change process is evident in SIP plan (e.g., limited initiatives, aligned focused professional development, integrated planning, related support structures). | 21. Evidence provided of adult learning or change process considered in planning. SIP tends to be fragmented with multiple initiatives, little attention to time requirements for implementation. |
| 22. Coaching/mentoring system creates a **coaching or mentoring cadre** by building capacity and application. | 22. Coaching/mentoring is planned and systemic. | 22. Coaching/mentoring is incidental. Viewed as sole responsibility of coach instead of schoolwide effort. |
| 23. Research-based instructional strategies, programs, and structures selected to impact **specified student needs** at school. ALL design activities and innovations are strongly correlated with student achievement gains. | 23. Majority of research-based instructional strategies, programs, and structures are linked to specified student needs at school (school, subgroup, or individual). | 23. Selected strategies, programs, and structures are not clearly linked to student needs evidenced by data. May lack support in research or best practice. |
| 24. Professional development (learning) that is **linked to meeting specific subgroup needs, addresses underlying causes** of any substandard performance, is limited to three major initiatives per goal, and prepares educators to improve decision-making through **planned reflection or analysis.** | 24. Professional development (learning) that is explicitly collaborative, selected to meet identified student needs (school, subgroup, or individual), embedded in functioning school processes, limited to three major initiatives per goal, and scheduled within normal school functions at least monthly. | 24. Fragmented professional development that may or may not address student needs at school. Professional development is rarely limited to three major initiatives per goal. Activities tend to be overly ambitious in number or scope. |
| 25. Support of professional development is provided for **ALL** initiatives in multiple ways (e.g., change procedures, cross-curricular applications or integration, subtract obsolete practices, collaboration, modeling). | 25. Support of professional development is provided in more than one way (change procedures, cross-curricular applications or integration, subtraction of obsolete practices, collaboration, modeling). | 25. Design has few systems to support professional development efforts. |

## Section E: Evaluation (5 practices)

| Exemplary: Score of 3 (All of 2 +) | Proficient: Score of 2 | Needs Improvement: Score of 1 |
|---|---|---|
| 26. **Evaluation compares planned with actual results in the prior year** and examines achievement results based on safety-net power standards by grade and compares them with district performance. Student comparisons are augmented by a specific review of curriculum impact, time/opportunity for students, or the effect of teaching practices on achievement. | 26. Evaluation summarizes data and evidence that examine student performance in multiple content areas and describes students in need of intervention whose performance puts them at risk of opening learning gaps. | 26. Evaluation tends to limit data summaries to student achievement analyses. Plans tend to examine student performance without specifying students in need of intervention whose performance puts them at risk of opening learning gaps. |
| 27. **Evaluation plan describes explicit new knowledge, specific skills, and attitudes** that will result from professional development associated with **each** goal for students, staff, **AND** stakeholders. | 27. Evaluation plan describes new knowledge and specific skills or attitudes that will result from professional development associated with the majority of goals for students and staff. | 27. Evaluation plan tends to describe new knowledge, skills, and attitudes in general terms and perceptions rather than specific knowledge or skills. |
| 28. **Evaluation specifies data and evidence needed to evaluate progress** in meeting all stated goals, including formative school-based Tier 2 data explicitly aligned to address those students whose performance puts them at risk of opening rather than closing learning gaps. | 28. Evaluation specifies data and evidence needed to evaluate progress to meet all stated goals, including formative school-based Tier 2 data and their frequency of collection. | 28. Evaluation tends to use identical generalities for each goal rather than to specify data and evidence needed to evaluate progress toward goals. |

| 29. Next steps are documented that outline how changes in teaching and learning will occur, describe how the leadership team analyzes data, provide evidence of submitting data to colleagues and peers for review, recommend changes from alternatives, and delineates a process to secure resources, implement changes, and evaluate results. | 29. Next steps to improve teaching and learning are delineated and supported by a clearly defined improvement cycle in the plan. | 29. Next steps rarely address changes in how teaching and learning will occur; next steps, if specified, tend to describe future outcome targets (goals) rather than next steps in terms of adult actions. |
|---|---|---|
| 30. Evaluation plan is **transparent** in describing how results (positive or negative), conclusions, lessons learned, and **next steps will be communicated and disseminated** to all primary stakeholders (families, educators, staff, patrons, partners, and the public). | 30. Plan describes how compared results (positive or negative) are communicated to improve goal-setting and ensure lessons learned. | 30. Evaluation plan may describe process for communicating results, but seldom specifies how results will be explained to stakeholders or describes next steps. |

| SUMMARY | Comprehensive Needs Assessment | Inquiry Process | SMART Goals | Design | Evaluation | Notes |
|---|---|---|---|---|---|---|
| Exemplary | | | | | | |
| Proficient | | | | | | |
| Needs Improvement | | | | | | |
| TOTAL SCORE: | | | | | | |

# Galileo's Dilemma

## The Illusion of Scientific Certainty
## in Educational Research

**A**S HE SURVEYED THE HEAVENS, Galileo made careful observations and challenged the prevailing hypothesis that the earth was the center of the universe. But this same scientist, so careful in his observations, also came to conclusions about the tides that were, by today's standards, laughably wrong. That the scientific method can be both illuminating and wrong, even when practiced by a distinguished researcher, is a cautionary tale for educators, school leaders, and policymakers.

As any observer of educational policy who has not been living in a cave knows, there are now federal mandates for the use of "scientific" programs in education. I know this because I have done what few members of Congress have done: I actually read the "No Child Left Behind" Act of 2001, signed into law by President Bush in January [2002] after passing Congress by overwhelming majorities. In its formidable 1,184 pages, the law uses the term "scientific" or "scientifically" 116 times and the word "research" 246 times. The current controversy over what "scientific research" means in the context of education implies a dichotomy between certainty and sophistry that exists only in the minds of partisans who appear to revel in yet another fact-free debate on educational policy. Let us separate myth from reality:

**MYTH NO. 1**  Science grants certainty. What does scientific research really mean? Does it, as its proponents imply, provide a world in which,

Reprinted from Douglas B. Reeves (2002), Galileo's dilemma: The illusion of scientific certainty in educational research. *Education Week, 21*(34), 33, 44.

if we only followed the salutary models of medicine, chemistry, and physics, rational people would agree on clear and obvious solutions? Or does it give us complexity and uncertainty, with debates over the effectiveness of mammography, the sequence of elements, and the number of planets in our solar system, along with the quandaries over tides and planetary bodies confronted by Galileo? When scientific methods are applied, researchers can disagree. They can even be wrong. Even in the hard sciences, controversies abound and certainty is elusive. While educators can learn much from scientific methods, the insinuation that these methods grant certitude is, to put it charitably, a hypothesis unsupported by the evidence.

**MYTH NO. 2**    Double-blind studies, such as those used in pharmaceutical research, are the gold standard for educational research. In pharmaceutical studies, the control group receives a placebo while the experimental group receives the real drug. In an astonishing number of cases, both groups show evidence of improved health. That is, something that researchers know to be valueless demonstrates an apparent impact on patient health. As a result, researchers do not have a clean line of demarcation between success and failure, but rather some evidence that some degree of health is associated with some dosage of the experimental medicine that is less evident in the absence of that drug. Where there is a relationship between the experimental medicine and improved health, researchers note that there is an association—a statistical correlation—between the drug and the condition of the patient. They cannot make conclusions about cause and effect until they have a detailed understanding of the physiology of the biochemical reactions caused by the medicine. Sometimes, as is the case with the origin of many cancers, correlation is all that scientists have, as the physiological evidence remains unavailable.

The most serious problem with pharmaceutical studies is that other variables, including the condition of the patient, nutrition, attitude, exercise, diet, sleep, and a host of other personal and environmental conditions that affect the medicine are not always perfectly controlled. Educational researchers, the presumed unscientific slugs in this debate, have not yet figured out how to control the nutrition, attitude, exercise, diet, and sleep of their research subjects, any more than they have figured out how to control the 18 hours each day spent outside of school.

**MYTH NO. 3**    The No Child Left Behind Act clearly defines scientific research. In fact, a reading of the plain language of the bill makes two inferences abundantly clear. First, the demand for scientifically supported programs, however pervasive, does not exist in a vacuum. Throughout the bill, the same sentence links a demand for such programs with an equally strong imperative for support of a broad and academically rigorous curriculum. In numerous instances, the same sentence links scientific programs with a demand for professional-development programs.

Most state standards require that 4th grade students comprehend the logic of Venn diagrams, in which students must understand that a statement can be part of one set but not necessarily represent a definition of the entire set. Participants in the debate over educational research would be well advised to rise to this standard. To put a fine point on it, the assertion that "science equals phonics" is only true with respect to the fact that some research studies support the use of phonics as part of an effective reading program. The assertion that "any program that does not include phonics is not scientific" does not meet the standard of logic we require of 4th graders.

**MYTH NO. 4**    Anything bearing the label "research" is worthy of the name. One need only recall the tobacco advertisements of the 1940s in which physicians endorsed the soothing effect of cigarettes on the throat to question the relationship between authority figures and putative research conclusions. Personal opinions, distorted case studies, and flimsy observations all masquerade as "research." Galileo's successors in the 19th and early 20th centuries used their version of science to prove the superiority of the Scandinavian over the Italian and the rightful subordination of the African to the European. Academic journals in the early days of the 21st century allow the inconveniences of sample size and detailed disclosure of experimental methods to give way to political agendas. Rather than be defensive, educators should acknowledge these problems, just as researchers in medicine, physics, and chemistry regularly air their dirty linen and, with equal amounts of clumsiness and rigor, advance the cause of reason.

In education, the mantras of "studies show" and "research proves" are the staple of too many vacuous keynote speakers for whom a footnote is a distant memory of a high school term paper. The real researchers I know confess that our work is but a pebble on a mountain of research begun by others, list the details of findings, welcome double-checks and criticism, and eat crow on a regular basis, firm in the conviction that transparent error is the price we pay for knowledge. Our mistakes involve more work and more risk than speculation unencumbered by evidence, and by our mistakes we simultaneously confess error and advance knowledge.

**THE FRAILTIES** of scientific research do not render us helpless. We can formulate sound opinions and make well-reasoned decisions on the allocation of scarce resources based on the information available. Rather than asserting that we have found ultimate truth with as much conviction as Galileo had in his false conclusions about ocean tides, we can acknowledge our limitations. The best we can do is consider a variety of conflicting studies and recognize the inherent uncertainties of research. At the same time, we must challenge the "scientifically based" assertions of others, particularly when prejudgment is substituted for fact.

Congress and the president got it right, though perhaps not in the way that they intended. We do need scientifically based programs in education. But real science involves ambiguity, experimentation, and error. However distasteful that trio may be, it is far superior to political agendas, uninformed prejudice, and breathless enthusiasm for the flavor of the month.

# Guidelines for Data Walls, or "The Science Fair for Grownups"

ONE OF THE MOST POWERFUL TECHNIQUES that educators and school leaders can use to improve decision-making in the classroom, school, and district is the "Data Wall." Ideally, the Data Wall is a portable display prepared on the cardboard three-panel display frequently used for student science fairs. When administrators gather to discuss their ideas for improving student achievement, Data Walls can provide a rich source of information about the strategies employed in each school. Within individual schools, Data Walls can be the focal point for faculty discussions on improving student achievement. For principals and teachers who are already using data to guide their instructional decision-making, the use of a Data Wall will not create significant additional work. For leaders who are not using data to guide their decisions, creation of Data Walls is a valuable technique for jump-starting their work. Most importantly, consistent application of this technique will ensure that the analysis of student data is not isolated to a single seminar or a staff development program on data, but rather becomes an ongoing part of faculty and administrative decision-making throughout the school year.

## Three Essential Parts of the Data Wall

1. External data (such as state test scores).
2. Internal data (classroom assessments or other school measurements involving teaching practices chosen by the school that reflect its unique needs).
3. Inferences and conclusions (drawn from the data).

# Information for the Panels

Each of the three panels of the Data Wall displays materials relevant to one of the three essential features listed above. For example, a Data Wall on strategies for improving student achievement in mathematics would include displays such as those described below.

**LEFT PANEL**  Includes tables, charts, and graphs that illustrate state test scores for the school and district. There may also be narrative comments, such as "84% of our students are proficient or higher in mathematics according to the state test scores, and 78% are proficient according to a district test. A review of the last three years of data shows consistent progress on both state and district measurements, with particular gains in the problem-solving portion of the math assessments."

**MIDDLE PANEL**  Includes data on teaching strategies associated with mathematics followed by another brief narrative, such as "The charts above show that the number of mathematics assessments including student writing has increased significantly in the past three years. Those assessments have emphasized the problem-solving portions of the state test. The charts also show a strong increase in interdisciplinary mathematics instruction, with the frequency of math instruction in music, art, physical education, technology, science, and social studies much greater for the most recent school year than was the case in earlier years."

**RIGHT PANEL**  Includes inferences and conclusions, such as "Our analysis of the data suggests that multidisciplinary instruction in math and writing in math have both been effective strategies to improve student performance. Therefore, we have planned to expand these strategies in the following ways: [provide examples of the strategies specifically applicable to the individual school]. We remain very concerned about the 16% of students who are not proficient on the math portion of the state tests, and we have developed individualized learning plans for each of these students. In addition, we have added the following intervention strategies for all non-proficient students: [include specific strategies applicable to your school]."

# Other Notes on Preparing for the "Science Fair for Grownups"

1. Principals will not make formal presentations—the Data Walls speak for themselves. Principals should be prepared to respond to questions from colleagues about their Data Walls.

2. The primary function of the Data Wall and Science Fair is to allow principals to ask one another questions and share with each other informally how they achieved their successes. If the Science Fair takes place during a multi-day leadership conference, then the displays should be set up during the breakfast of the first day and left up throughout the conference.

3. The process of continuous collaboration must continue all year, not just at a retreat or seminar. The Data Walls can be the focus of internal staff development, joint faculty meetings with other schools, and planning for instructional interventions and professional development activities.

4. ***Critically Important:*** The Data Walls are not for the purpose of impressing outside observers, the superintendent, or any other external audience. The primary purpose of the Data Walls is for the principals to share information with their fellow principals and, most importantly, with their faculties.

5. Principals will have to make choices regarding which data to use. They will want to show the information that is most important, drawing clear conclusions, and making the point to the faculty members that they are not merely *displaying* data, but *using* data to inform their leadership decision-making.

# Science Fair Reflections

## "The Treasure Hunt"

Name: _____

Date: _____

1. Identify one or two important challenges that you face with regard to improving student achievement and educational equity:



2. Find one or two other displays illustrate a challenge similar to one of your challenges, but that appeared to have better results.

   What did you notice that was *similar* in the strategies that were used in the other displays?



   What did you notice that was *different* in the strategies that were used in the other displays?

What did you notice about the ***results***? How are the results related to the strategies?

3. *Data Analysis and Displays:* What did you notice about the data display that you can use to improve your displays for the next Science Fair? Identify two or three specific best practices in the display and communication of information:

4. *Action Plan:* Based on what you have learned during this Science Fair, what are your most important priorities with regard to refining strategies, communicating information, and achieving results?

5. *Recommended Improvements:* How can the next version of the Science Fair be improved to make this event most useful for you and the schools that you serve?

---

Your feedback and reflections are very important. Please turn in one complete copy of this form before you leave the Science Fair today.

Thank you!

# References

Ainsworth, L., & Viegut, D. (2006). *Common formative assessments: How to connect standards-based instruction and assessment.* Thousand Oaks, CA: Corwin Press.

Amabile, T. M., & Kramer, S. J. (2010, January–February). What really motivates workers. *Harvard Business Review, 88*(1), 44–45.

Berman, S. (2008, October). A superintendent's systemic notion of civics. *The School Administrator, 65*(9), 29–31.

Campbell, D. T., & Stanley, J. C. (1963). *Experimental and quasi-experimental designs for research.* Chicago: Rand McNally.

Carbonneau, N., Vallerand, R. J., Fernet C., & Guay, F. (2008, November). The role of passion for teaching in intrapersonal and interpersonal outcomes. *Journal of Educational Psychology, 100*(4), 977–987.

Casciaro, T., & Lobo, M. S. (2005, June). Competent jerks, lovable fools, and the formation of social networks. *Harvard Business Review, 83*(6), 92–99, 149.

Colvin, G. (2008). *Talent is overrated: What really separates world-class performers from everybody else.* New York: Portfolio.

Darling-Hammond, L. (2000). Teacher quality and student achievement: A review of state policy evidence. *Educational Policy Analysis Archives, 8*(1), 1–50.

Darwin, C. Quoted at Environmental Protection Agency, Science Quotes. Retrieved October 13, 2010, from http://www.epa.gov/yearofscience/quotes.htm

Deutchman, A. (2007). *Change or die: The three keys to change at work and in life.* New York: HarperCollins.

Erickson, J. A. (2010, March). Grading practices: The third rail. *Principal Leadership, 10*(7), 22–26.

Fullan, M. (2005). *Leadership & sustainability: System thinkers in action.* Thousand Oaks, CA: Corwin Press.

Fullan, M. (2008a). *The six secrets of change: What the best leaders do to help their organizations survive and thrive.* San Francisco: Jossey-Bass.

Fullan, M. (2008b). *What's worth fighting for in the principalship?* New York: Teachers College Press.

Fullan, M. (2009). *Motion leadership: The skinny on becoming change savvy.* Thousand Oaks, CA: Corwin Press.

Fullan, M. (2010). *All systems go: The change imperative for whole system reform.* Thousand Oaks, CA: Corwin Press.

Galbraith, J. K. (1989, July 28). Quoted in *The Guardian* (UK).

Gallagher, W. (2009). *Rapt: Attention and the focused life.* New York: Penguin Group.

Goodlad, J. I. (1984). *A place called school: Prospects for the future.* New York: McGraw-Hill.

Goodlad, J. I. (1990). *Teachers for our nation's schools.* San Francisco: Jossey-Bass.

Greenleaf, R. K., Spears, L. C., & Covey, S. R. (2002). *Servant leadership: A journey into the nature of legitimate power and greatness.* Mahwah, NJ: Paulist Press.

Guskey, T. R. (2000). *Evaluating professional development.* Thousand Oaks, CA: Corwin Press.

Guskey, T. R., & Bailey, J. M. (2001). *Developing grading and reporting systems for student learning.* Thousand Oaks, CA: Corwin Press.

Hamel, G. (2009, February). Moon shots for management. *Harvard Business Review, 87*(2), 91–98.

Hargreaves, A., & Fink, D. (2006). *Sustainable leadership.* San Francisco: Jossey-Bass.

Hargreaves, A., & Fullan, M. (Eds.). (2009). *Change wars.* Bloomington, IN: Solution Tree.

Hattie, J. (2009). *Visible learning: A synthesis of over 800 meta-analyses relating to achievement.* New York: Routledge.

Haycock, K. (1998, Summer). Good teaching matters . . . a lot. *The Education Trust, 3*(2), 3–14.

Ingersoll, R., & Perda, D. (2009). *How high is teacher turnover and is it a problem?* Consortium for Policy Research in Education, University of Pennsylvania.

Kim, J.-O., & Mueller, C. W. (1978). *Factor analysis: Statistical methods and practical issues.* Beverly Hills, CA: Sage.

Kim, W. C., & Mauborgne, R. (2005). *Blue ocean strategy: How to create uncontested market space and make the competition irrelevant.* Boston: Harvard Business School Press.

Kiuhara, S. A., Graham, S., & Hawken, L. S. (2009, February). Teaching writing to high school students: A national survey. *Journal of Educational Psychology, 101*(1), 136–160.

Kohn, A. (2006). *The homework myth: Why our kids get too much of a bad thing.* Cambridge, MA: Da Capo Press.

Kotter, J. P. (2008). *A sense of urgency.* Boston: Harvard Business School Press.

Levin, B. (2008). *How to change 5000 schools: A practical and positive approach for leading change at every level.* Cambridge, MA: Harvard Education Press.

Marshall, K. (2010). *Rethinking teacher supervision and evaluation: How to work smart, build collaboration, and close the achievement gap.* San Francisco: Jossey-Bass.

Marzano, R. J. (2003). *What works in schools: Translating research into action.* Alexandria, VA: Association for Supervision and Curriculum Development.

Marzano, R. J. (2006). *Classroom assessment and grading that work.* Alexandria, VA: Association for Supervision and Curriculum Development.

Marzano, R. J. (2007). *The art and science of teaching: A comprehensive framework for effective instruction.* Alexandria, VA: Association for Supervision and Curriculum Development.

Marzano, R. J. (2009a). *Formative assessment and standards-based grading: Classroom strategies that work.* Bloomington, IN: Solution Tree.

Marzano, R. J. (2009b, September). Setting the record straight on "high-yield" strategies. *Phi Delta Kappan, 91*(1), 30–37.

Marzano, R. J., & Kendall, J. S. (1998). *Awash in a sea of standards.* Aurora, CO: Mid-continent Research for Education and Learning.

Marzano, R. J., & Pickering, D. (2007). The case for and against homework. *Educational Leadership, 64*(6), 74–79.

Marzano, R. J., Pickering, D., & Pollock, J. E. (2001). *Classroom instruction that works: Research-based strategies for increasing student achievement.* Alexandria, VA: Association for Supervision and Curriculum Development.

Marzano, R. J., & Waters, T. W. (2009). *District leadership that works: Striking the right balance.* Bloomington, IN: Solution Tree.

Marzano, R. J., Waters, T., & McNulty, B. A. (2005). *School leadership that works: From research to results.* Alexandria, VA: Association for Supervision and Curriculum Development.

McKean, E. (Ed). (2005). *The new Oxford American dictionary* (2nd ed.). New York: Oxford University Press.

Milgram, S. (1974). *Obedience to authority: An experimental view.* New York: Harper and Row.

National Governors Association (NGA) & The Council of Chief State School Officers (CCSSO). (2010). *Common Core State Standards.* http://www.corestandards.org/

Oberman, I., & Symonds, K. W. (2005). What matters most in closing the gap. *Leadership, 34*(3), 8–11.

Patterson, K., Grenny, J., Maxfield, D., McMillan, R., & Switzler, A. (2008). *Influencer: The power to change anything.* New York: McGraw-Hill.

Peters, T. J., & Waterman, R. H., Jr. (1982). *In search of excellence: Lessons from America's best-run companies.* New York: Warner Books.

Pink, D. H. (2009). *Drive: The surprising truth about what motivates us.* New York: Riverhead Books.

Popham, W. J. (2008). *Transformative assessment.* Alexandria, VA: Association for Supervision and Curriculum Development.

Porter, M. (1980). *Competitive strategy: Techniques for analyzing industries and competitors.* New York: Free Press.

Reeves, D. B. (2002a). *The daily disciplines of leadership: How to improve student achievement, staff motivation, and personal organization.* San Francisco: Jossey-Bass.

Reeves, D. B. (2002b). Galileo's dilemma: The illusion of scientific certainty in educational research. *Education Week, 21*(34), 33, 44.

Reeves, D. B. (2002c). *The leader's guide to standards: A blueprint for educational equity and excellence.* San Francisco: Jossey-Bass.

Reeves, D. B. (2006a). *The learning leader: How to focus school improvement for better results.* Alexandria, VA: Association for Supervision and Curriculum Development.

Reeves, D. B. (2006b, November). Preventing 1,000 failures. *Educational Leadership, 64*(3), 88–89.

Reeves, D. B. (2007, November). How do you sustain excellence? *Educational Leadership, 65*(3), 86–87.

Reeves, D. B. (2008a). *Reframing teacher leadership to improve your school.* Alexandria, VA: Association for Supervision and Curriculum Development.

Reeves, D. B. (2008b, February). Effective grading practices. *Educational Leadership,* 65(5), 85–87.

Reeves, D. B. (2008c, May). Improving student attendance. *Educational Leadership,* 65(8), 90–91.

Reeves, D. B. (2008, December–2009, January). Looking deeper into the data. *Educational Leadership, 66*(4), 89–90.

Reeves, D. B. (2009a). *Assessing educational leaders: Evaluating performance for improved individual and organizational results* (2nd ed.). Thousand Oaks, CA: Corwin Press.

Reeves, D. B. (2009b). *Leading change in your school: How to conquer myths, build commitment, and get results.* Alexandria, VA: Association for Supervision and Curriculum Development.

Reeves, D. B. (2010). *Elements of grading: A guide to effective practice.* Bloomington, IN: Solution Tree.

Reeves, D. B., & Allison, E. (2009). *Renewal coaching: Sustainable change for individuals and organizations.* San Francisco: Jossey-Bass.

Rosenthal, R., & Jacobson, L. (2003). *Pygmalion in the classroom: Teacher expectation and pupil's intellectual development.* Carmarthen, UK: Crown House.

Rothstein, R. (2004a). *Class and schools: Using social, economic, and educational reform to close the Black–White achievement gap.* Washington, DC: Economic Policy Institute.

Rothstein, R. (2004b). Class and the classroom: Even the best schools can't close the race achievement gap. *American School Board Journal, 191*(10), 16.

Schmoker, M. J. (2004). Tipping point: From feckless reform to substantive instructional improvement. *Phi Delta Kappan, 85*(6), 424–432.

Schmoker, M. (2006). *Results now: How we can achieve unprecedented improvements in teaching and learning.* Alexandria, VA: Association for Supervision and Curriculum Development.

Smith, L. (2008). *Schools that change evidence-based improvement and effective change leadership.* Thousand Oaks, CA: Corwin Press.

Twain, M. Quoted at Quote DB. Retrieved October 18, 2010, from http://www.quote db.com/quotes/1097

*Video Journal of Education.* (1999). Volume 1001. Sandy, UT: School Information Network.

Wiggins, G. (1998). *Educative assessment: Designing assessments to inform and improve student performance.* San Francisco: Jossey-Bass.

# Index

# About the Author

**DOUGLAS B. REEVES** is the founder of The Leadership and Learning Center. He has worked with education, business, nonprofit, and government organizations throughout the world. The author of more than 20 books and many articles on leadership and organizational effectiveness, he has twice been named to the Harvard University Distinguished Authors Series.

Reeves was named the Brock International Laureate for his contributions to education. He also received the Distinguished Service Award from the National Association of Secondary School Principals and the Parents' Choice Award for his writing for children and parents, and he is a recipient of the National Staff Development Council's Contributions to the Field Award for 2010.